Copyright © 1982 Lion Publishing,
England

First American edition 1982
**William B. Eerdmans Publishing
Company**
255 Jefferson Ave., S.E., Grand Rapids,
Michigan, 49503
ISBN 0 8028 3575 9

First edition 1982

Printed and bound in Hong Kong by
Mandarin Offset International (HK) Ltd.

3.83 Baker 11.66

Photographs are reproduced by
permission of the following
photographers and organizations, and
with grateful thanks to the congregations
of the churches shown:

The Architectural Association, Peter
Minchin, 87 (below), 90
Architectural Press, 91 (above)
Mervyn Benford, 34, 78 (centre)
Stephen Benson Slide Bureau, 91 (centre)
Brecht-Einzig, 89 (below)
Simon Bull, 40 (right), 49 (below)
Camera Press, cover (above right), 60 (left)
Paul Clowney, 49 (above), 62
The Dutch Tourist Board, 45 (below right),
61 (above left), 82 (left), 83 (above)
Mary Evans Picture Library, 50, 53 (left),
55 (left), 68, 84 (above)
Fritz Fankhauser, 78 (below)
Jeffrey Fewkes, 87 (above)
The French Government Tourist Office,
41 (above), 43 (below), 45 (below left), 51,
60 (right)
The German Tourist Office, 42 (left),
58 (both)
Sonia Halliday Photographs, cover
(below, both), 35, 36, 37 (above), 59, 64
(left), 65, 66–67 (all), 85; Jane Taylor, 71,
76–77
Hamlyn Group Picture Library, 73 (below
right)
Michael Holford, 73 (below left), 83
(below), back endpapers
Paul Kay, 21 (above right), 89 (above)
Lion Publishing; David Alexander, 30, 42
(right), 50, 53 (right), 70, 75; David Vesey,
21 (below left); Jon Willcocks, cover
(above centre), front endpaper, 5 (all), 11,
12 (both), 13 (both), 14, 15, 20 (left), 21
(above right, below right), 24 (below left,
below centre), 25 (both), 26, 27 (all),
28 (both), 29, 38, 39 (above), 41 (below),
43 (above, both), 46–47 (all), 48, 52 (both),
55 (right), 56, 57 (both), 61 (below right),
63, 64 (right), 74 (above left), 77 (right),
78 (above), 79 (below), 80–81, 80 (left),
91 (below)
Wulf Metz, 84 (below)
David Morgan, 54, 61 (below left)
Press-tige Photos, 11–12
Ronald Sheridan, cover (left), 24 (below
right), 33, 37 (below), 39 (below), 40 (left)
The Swedish Tourist Board, 44 (all), 88
(left)
Derek Walker Associates, 76 (below left),
82 (right)
Western Americana Picture Library, 73
(above), 79 (above), 81 (right)
Liam White, 20 (right)
Derek Widdicombe, 74 (above right)

Line drawings by Simon Bull

Diagrams
Dick Barnard, 16–17, 18 (left), 18–19,
20–21
Paul Jones, 15 (right), 19 (above), 24–25
Roy Lawrence, 22–23, 29
David Reddick, 31, 32, 37, 70
Stanley Willcocks, 15 (left), 19 (right), 33,
51, 57
Daniel Woods, 6, 7, 8, 9

Pages 2–11 Milan Cathedral

EXPLORING CHURCHES

Paul & Tessa Clowney

William B. Eerdmans Publishing Company
Grand Rapids, Michigan

CONTENTS

PART 2
THE STORY OF CHURCH BUILDING

INTRODUCTION

The word 'church' can mean two different things: a building – or people. First and foremost, in fact, it means a group of people who have been called together by God to form the 'body' of those who share new life through Jesus Christ. A group of Russian Christians meeting in secret in a home is just as much a 'church' as a massive cathedral congregation.

But the word has also come to be used of the buildings in which the church meets. And so the buildings can help us to understand something of the motives of the original builders, the way the building has been used, and the beliefs it expresses.

Churches and cathedrals often form the peak of an age's architectural output. Whether built for the glory of God or of men, they represent a staggering commitment of time, skill and money, and were built by the foremost craftsmen of the day, often employing the most up-to-date building techniques. So simply as buildings, the heritage of churches and cathedrals is awe-inspiring. Exploring churches means enjoying centuries of cultural history. And sometimes the smallest church can be just as fascinating as the biggest cathedral.

But as well as being architecturally fascinating, each church reveals maybe hundreds of years of Christian history. Succeeding generations have used the building in different ways, in keeping with their changing understanding of the Christian faith. And each generation has left its mark on the building. An eleventh-century building, for example, might have been expanded in the Middle Ages, with the clergy's chancel entirely separate from the people's nave; in the Reformation screens, statues and paintings would have been cleared out; in the eighteenth century a new organ might have been fitted and a hundred years later new floors and heating; in the last twenty years all the pews might have been replaced by chairs and the altar moved from the east end to the

centre of the building. All these changes can be read in the fabric of building.

The second section of this book, The Story of Church Building, examines why different styles of building developed. In most cases the design of a church is a reflection of the way the people of the time understood God and their fellow men, and the way in which services of worship were conducted – whether the clergy said all the words, or the congregation took part, whether there was a procession or not, where the communion table was placed, and so on.

Churches were usually designed with a particular form of service or 'liturgy' in mind. An Eastern Orthodox church separates the priest from the people behind a solid screen. A Quaker meeting-house consists of simple benches facing each other – for there is no 'priest' at all. If the liturgy changed, the building sometimes had to be changed, too. The building itself could also affect the liturgy. Cavernous medieval churches had peculiar acoustics, for example, and to cope with them, it became customary to chant the service.

The first part, the Fieldguide, is intended to be a practical guide to the building and its use. It concentrates mainly on ancient churches as being of most interest to tourists. But many of the same features will be found in different forms of church buildings generally. The section also helps in dating the building and understanding its various parts.

It is worth having a good look at the outside of the building first. The architect will have given a great deal of thought to the overall impression the building gives. If it is an old town church, you may have to 'think away' the surrounding buildings before you can appreciate the church as it first was – with fresh clean stone.

Going inside, first impressions are of great importance. Was the church designed to evoke awe, or mystery? How do the people who meet here week by week feel in the building? Colour, light and acoustics all go to make up this emotional impact of the building. As you explore the inside of the building, it pays to be systematic, 'understanding' first the nave, then the transepts and finally the choir and chancel. Compare the different parts of the building with each other. Are they all of the same period? How does the building compare with the last one you visited?

Then look at the details: the windows, the columns, the doorways, the furnishings. Are there the tell-tale hints of changes in belief or practice, for instance – statues defaced, chapels added, arches filled in?

It is instructive to notice how the church building is used today. Is it a museum or a meeting place? Some seem to be little more than showcases of religious history, full of exhibits, postcards and money-boxes. Others demonstrate a faith that is as alive today as ever.

Exploring churches is a pastime which becomes more and more intriguing. The variety is inexhaustible. This book is a guide to help you see and ask questions. Perhaps it will help you touch, smell, hear and imagine history as you enjoy the design of places of worship. Perhaps too it will help take you beyond the building to a better understanding of the faith that the building was designed to express.

PART 1
FIELDGUIDE

Outside the Building

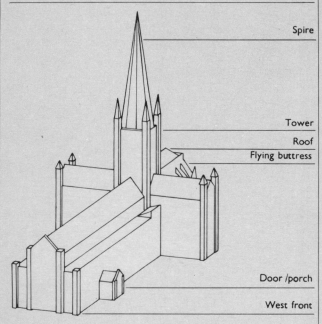

- Spire
- Tower
- Roof
- Flying buttress
- Door /porch
- West front

Towers

Building towers is not easy, as anyone who has tried to build sand castle knows. Towers require carefully-positioned foundations, a good deal of bracing, and well-fitted components. Sometimes they still collapse. In the late Middle Ages when tower building was almost a community competition, towers often fell. Considerable ingenuity has been applied through the centuries to propping up towers and spires. Iron bands, internal truss rods, strainer arches, additional flying buttresses – some towers have them all. And there are some remarkably crooked towers which do still manage to stand.

The obvious functions of a tower are to extend the range from which the church is visible and to support bells. Cathedrals have as many as nine towers, but the two most common arrangements are a single tower at the west end, and two towers on either side of the west front with a third large tower at the crossing. This

The huge tower of the church at Widecombe in the west of England.

central tower represents the church's contact between heaven and earth. Every effort has been made to keep the tower as light as possible; large windows and arches serve to reduce the weight. Towers have often been rebuilt or extended in later periods – not always with a happy marriage of styles.

West Fronts

The most considered exterior feature of larger churches and cathedrals is generally the west front. Medieval builders thought of this façade, incorporating the large entrance doors, as a symbol of the gate to heaven. As such it was more elaborately designed than any part of the building save the altar screen. The structure of the west front sometimes emphasizes the shape of the building behind it; sometimes it disguises it. The twin-tower façade which became the norm in the eleventh century divides the west end into three vertical sections, echoing the internal division of two aisles and a nave. A large window almost always fills the upper central part, sometimes balanced by openings in the flanking towers.

Because it was normal practice to begin building a church at the east end, the west is often dated later than the rest of the church. At times this difference is visible in a marked

The west front of Salisbury cathedral is dominated by the massive spire behind.

change in style. For example, west-end towers were regularly carried higher in later centuries. A Romanesque pediment surmounted by a Gothic tower and Baroque spire is not uncommon.

Norwich Cathedral, though bigger than any parish church, shows the typical cross-shaped plan of European Gothic churches. On the south side are the shaded cloisters: from its beginning, the cathedral had a monastery attached.

Spires

Not all churches have spires. Sometimes this is intentional design. In other cases the spire has been removed, has collapsed or has burnt after being struck by lightning. The spire has often been seen as a symbol of man's aspiration to be united with his creator. It was also a symbol of local pride, and a signpost for travellers. The building of a tall spire made tremendous demands on the finances and skills of a church. The easiest method was to build in timber and then clad with lead or copper; the wind stresses on such a construction are enormous, however, and so this sort of spire had to be drawn tightly down against the tower. If the foundations could take the weight, a spire could be built of stone, but this was expensive, dangerous and difficult. Each stone had to be carefully cut in compound angles, carried up the scaffolding, supported by templates and finally mortared into place.

The small spires or pinnacles at the base of the main central spire of a cathedral were more than decoration. By their extra weight they secured the base of the spire against the outward thrust.

Sites

Churches were often built on an important site – the grave of a martyr, or the site of a previous church. Not all of these locations were really ideal. The churches of Ravenna, Winchester and Ely were all built on marshland. Amsterdam required foundation piles driven as deep as the churches are tall. Subsidence in Ravenna has amounted to more than three feet (one metre) in places. Modern city life poses a serious threat to many old buildings; exhaust fumes erode the stone, vibrations from heavy traffic loosen the joints, excavations in the vicinity can affect foundations.

Many churches are built on hillsides, naturally dominating the area around.

Roofs

Roofs are often covered in lead plate, sometimes as much as a quarter of an inch (almost a centimetre) thick. The considerable weight of such a roof prevents it from being blown away but adds substantially to the stress on the walls. A carefully cross-braced beam structure lies between the roof cladding and the vault of the ceiling, and this forest of wood always adds to the hazard of fire. There are terrifying accounts of cathedral fires in which molten lead poured from the guttering like water.

The massive cathedral of Milan is roofed in great slabs of marble – sloping gently enough for people to walk on with ease.

Gargoyles

On a large roof, rain-water can pose problems. Simply getting rid of all the water from a cloudburst calls for careful design. If water overflows onto the walls or the vault it can cause rot or even collapse. The simplest way of getting rid of the water quickly was to fix great projecting spouts to the guttering so that the water could fall clear of the walls. These spouts commonly assumed the form of fantastic beasts called gargoyles.

Doors/Porches

The entrance doors of the west front of cathedrals were reserved for processions, state occasions and religious festivals. Day-to-day traffic entered in most cases through a doorway on the north-west aisle. This doorway was protected from the weather by a porch. The porch itself acquired a certain significance. Marriages were sometimes conducted there, and it was a common place to seal business agreements – 'by church door'.

There is some noteworthy sculpture in these porches, with two themes being particularly popular. The first is the baptism of Christ, for baptism is the symbol of entry into God's family, the church. The second theme is the changing seasons and their respective labours; this serves to remind the faithful that Christ is involved in all parts of human life.

As well as providing shelter at the door, the porch was used in medieval times for weddings and for trade.

Buttresses

Churches often have thickened sections of wall or even what look like small walls running out from the main building. The one purpose of these 'buttresses' is to give greater rigidity to the whole structure. The greater the weight of a buttress, the more it pushes down and the greater the lateral forces it can withstand.

The massive buttresses of Romanesque churches strengthened the fabric of the building but left little room for large windows. The Gothic builders, by contrast, placed buttresses only at key structural points. The further a buttress is from the wall it supports, the greater its efficiency. The best-constructed buttresses (and interior piers) are solid throughout. But it was simpler and cheaper to make them hollow and to fill the interior with rubble.

The structural strength of tall towers and walls is provided by carefully-placed buttresses.

Flying Buttresses

Flying buttresses are strengthening arches which reach from a vertical buttress to a wall, generally to the upper wall of the nave. These counteract the outward thrust of the roof against the comparatively thin upper nave wall.

The aisle, with its low roof, has a thick buttress outside it. On top of this are two levels of flying buttress which support the nave wall and bear outwards on a pinnacled column.

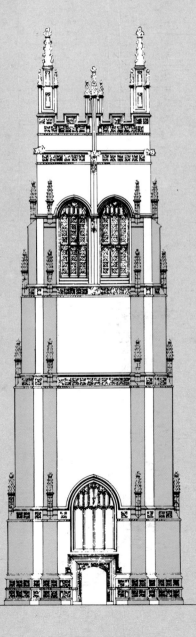

Bells

A full 'peal' of bells can weigh several tonnes, considerably adding to the weight of the tower. In the seventeenth century much ingenuity went into designing mechanical contrivances such as 'carillons' which could chime the bells. These are still used widely on the continent of Europe. In Britain 'change ringing' is more popular; the six or more bells are rung in intricately varying sequences.

15

Inside the Building

The Crossing

The intersection of the nave and the transept, the crossing, is a natural centre for a church. It is also the structural kingpin of the building. Here the space opens out in all directions and light from the nave mixes with light from the transept. In some larger churches there is a 'triforium', sometimes a passage-way which runs right round the transept. Get up into this space to look down on the crossing if you can possibly do so. The four corner piers of the crossing are thicker than the piers of the nave arcade. Occasionally arches are partially or completely blocked in to give the crossing greater strength. In some cases 'strainer arches' have been built in. But despite all the bracing and strainer arches, crossing towers and spires have sometimes still fallen through the roof.

The Transept

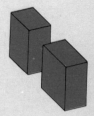

The transept crosses the nave at right angles. It gives the church the form of a cross. Some bigger churches have several transepts, sometimes diminishing in length towards the eastern end. The end walls of the transepts can be treated in many ways, but the most common is to have a 'blind arcading' – arches built nearly flush with the wall – sometimes with a large rose window above.

The Nave

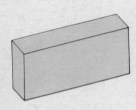

The nave (from 'navis' = ship) is the main area for the congregation. In medieval times it was a popular meeting-place, even for trading. The length of the nave is divided into bays by 'piers' or columns. Shafts which extend up the surface of the wall from the piers or columns are called 'half shafts' because of their semicircular cross section. These vertical divisions are almost always stressed in Gothic architecture to emphasize height. (If they run from vault to floor in an unbroken line they will emphasize the vertical more than if they stop at the top of the arcade; if the piers are composed of 'bundles' of shafts this also contributes to a vertical stress.)

The Aisles

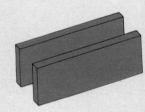

Aisles run parallel with the nave, often separated from it by the main columns. Generally the roof is lower over the aisles; the nave walls above the level of the aisle roofs are pierced with the clerestory windows. Aisles are mainly used for seating, but there may also be memorial tombs, as well as bookstalls and displays showing the work of the church and the missionary outreach it supports.

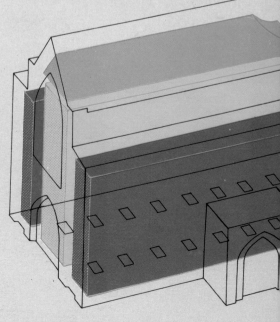

The Chancel/ Choir

The choir or chancel is where services are sung or said. To emphasize the mystery and holiness of the service in Catholic churches, the choir was often separated from the people by a screen. These screens are sometimes beautifully carved – the wood carver's flamboyant challenge to the stone worker. In addition to the screens the choir is also distinguished from the nave by a raised floor; in cases where churches were built over crypts, the level of the choir floor could be six to ten feet (two to three metres) higher than the nave. In the Middle Ages some choirs would be opened at stated times to allow pilgrims to view relics.

The Vault

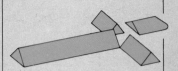

The vault or ceiling is always one of the more spectacular interior elements. From the crudely-hewn tunnel vaults of early Romanesque to the bizarre and gravity-defying pendulum vaults of the seventeenth century, these stone ceilings are always fascinating. The first rib vaults in the twelfth century were a functional solution to the roofing problem. It was not long before ribs were being used for a decorative effect as well as for structural purposes. Short rib sections spread from the tops of half shafts like a net over the nave, each intersection embellished by a carved and painted boss. Vaults were often added later; it was common practice to roof first in timber. Sometimes a later vault does not fit in neatly with the clerestory.

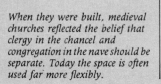

When they were built, medieval churches reflected the belief that clergy in the chancel and congregation in the nave should be separate. Today the space is often used far more flexibly.

Nave Levels

Naves are often built in three 'layers'; at the bottom the large arched arcade; then the middle level of arches, the triforium. Above this is the clerestory – windows over the aisle roof which let light into the nave. Sometimes a fourth division called a **tribune** is added. The proportions of the different levels were the subject of extensive discussion. If the span of the arches in the triforium is too broad compared to their height, the middle section of the wall can seem a bit squashed!

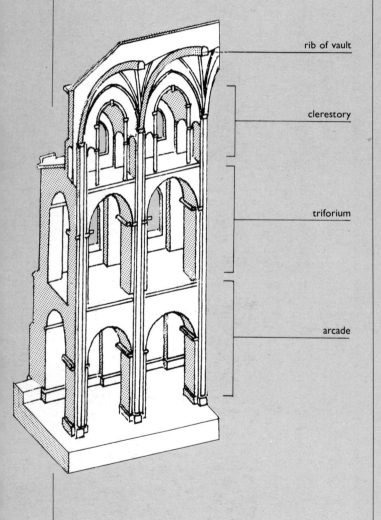

rib of vault

clerestory

triforium

arcade

Capitals

The capitals, or tops of the columns, are usually carved with foliage, figures, patterns, or all three. Note the way in which the shape of the capital is harmonized with the figures. Such carving required experience – if the chisel broke a bit off there was no option but to change the design or to start again.

In this example, the triforium forms a passage right round the building, almost the size of the aisle below it. The round-headed arches show that the nave was built in the Norman period. The pointed windows in the chancel date from the fifteenth century.

Chapels

Small chapels are often built off the eastern wall of transepts and on side-aisles. Many of these were 'chantry chapels'; they were commissioned in the Middle Ages by the wealthy for the 'chanting' of daily mass on behalf of the souls of members of their family who had died, in the belief that prayers could reduce their time in purgatory. Today they are used for private prayer, for smaller services, or as places for people to come to 'confession', unburdening their sins with a spiritual adviser.

The Ambulatory

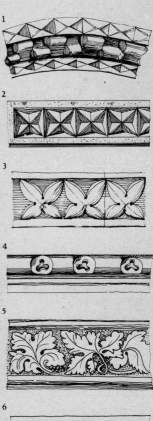

The passage which runs around and behind the choir is known as the ambulatory, for 'walking round'. In the more prestigious plans twin ambulatories were popular; it was a particularly suitable arrangement for pilgrim churches. The usual treatment of the eastern end of the building in Europe was the chevet or half circle of chapels opening off the bays of a rounded apse. In England there is sometimes a 'Lady Chapel' – usually in the form of a highly decorated extension to the east end of the choir, dedicated to the Virgin Mary.

Moulding

Moulding is sometimes cut from contrasting stone. The horizontal divisions are usually stressed with thin stone mouldings known as stringing. Compare cross-sections of the piers, window mullions (the vertical dividers) with half-shafts, stringing, ribs, and so on. These stones were cut from 'profile templates', so looking at cross-sections shows how the architect achieved his goal.

Some styles of moulding have their own names. The 'billet and lozenge' (1) and the 'star' (2) date from the eleventh century, the 'ballflower' (4) and 'vine' (5) from the high Gothic period. (3) also dates from this period, and (6) from the late Gothic.

The Building in Use

The activities of a particular church are represented in the building that has been developed over the years to serve its various purposes.

The local church or chapel is usually built as the meeting place of a local congregation, used for services for worship Sunday by Sunday, for festivals such as Christmas and Easter, for Sunday schools for children and many other purposes. There is plenty of seating for the congregation.

Cathedrals

The Cathedral, usually in a city centre, is the central building of a diocese – the church's 'area headquarters', led by the bishop. Often it is used for more formal and civic occasions. Particularly if there is a choir school, there is stress on services being sung or said on behalf of the community rather than with the involvement of the congregation.

Congregation ①

The congregation sits in pews or seats usually facing one end; or in modern churches and those stressing communal fellowship they may be gathered round a central communion table.

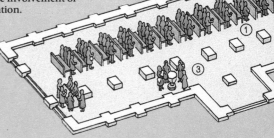

Festivals

Festivals such as Christmas and Easter are celebrated in local churches and cathedrals. **Christmas** celebrates the birth of Jesus; card services, candlelit services and other traditions make it a joyful festival, often involving the children. **Easter** recalls the death and resurrection of Jesus: Good Friday is an opportunity for repentance and renewed forgiveness; Easter Day the triumphant celebration of the rising again of Jesus to new life as the first of a new creation. **Whitsun** remembers the coming of the Spirit of God to the church. Other festivals such as **Harvest** bring thanksgiving to God; all are opportunities for decorating the church in imaginative and appropriate ways.

Private Chapels ②

Private chapels were often built at the end of the medieval period or in the nineteenth century to say masses on behalf of a wealthy individual, not for congregational use at all. Side-chapels in cathedrals sometimes represent the same belief and practice. Reformed churches discontinued the practice, as it undermined their teaching that salvation is by trust in the work of Jesus, not anything we can do for ourselves.

THIS PAGE, LEFT *In this packed Baptist church at Christmas the gallery gives a good view of the children's nativity play.* ABOVE *The cathedral is used not just for services but also for events such as this international gathering of young people.* OPPOSITE, ABOVE LEFT *Baptism in this church is by 'total immersion'.* BELOW RIGHT *In an Anglican church, the minister leading the service gives bread and wine to the congregation.*

Baptism ③

Baptism is a vivid visual demonstration of becoming a Christian. The person 'dies' to his old sinful life by going down into water, and 'rises again with Jesus' in newness of life. Some churches practice this quite literally with a large 'baptistry' which allows people to go right into the water. In other churches a stone 'font' fulfils the same function more symbolically, and the water is sprinkled. In the case of children, promises are made by parents or god-parents on behalf of the child which are later 'confirmed' if the person comes to full belief.

Choirs ⑤

The choir lead the singing from the chancel or choir-stalls, usually accompanied by an **organ.** Hymns and psalms are a major part of services. In some churches the whole service is sung: in medieval times the voice would carry to a very large congregation if the service was intoned or sung.

Priory, convent or monastery churches are designed for the daily services of a community of Christians who live together. Sometimes they require only the 'chancel' or choir part of the church, as there is no other congregation, so no need for the main nave at all – except for churches at a place of pilgrimage.

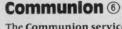

Communion ⑥

The **Communion service, Mass, Eucharist, Lord's Supper** (varying names for the same service) is usually a main event in the church's life. It is a 'visual aid' of the death and rising again of Jesus: just as bread and wine are shared, believers share in forgiveness for their sins by the death of Jesus, and in new life by his rising again. It is celebrated from a communion table; sometimes a simple wooden table, or in churches which stress the service as a re-enactment of Jesus' sacrifice a stone or marble altar. In some churches different coloured altar-cloths are used at different times in the church's year.

Sunday Schools ④

A Sunday school often has a corner or room in a church: children are taught in classes appropriate to their age-group.

Main Periods of Church Architecture

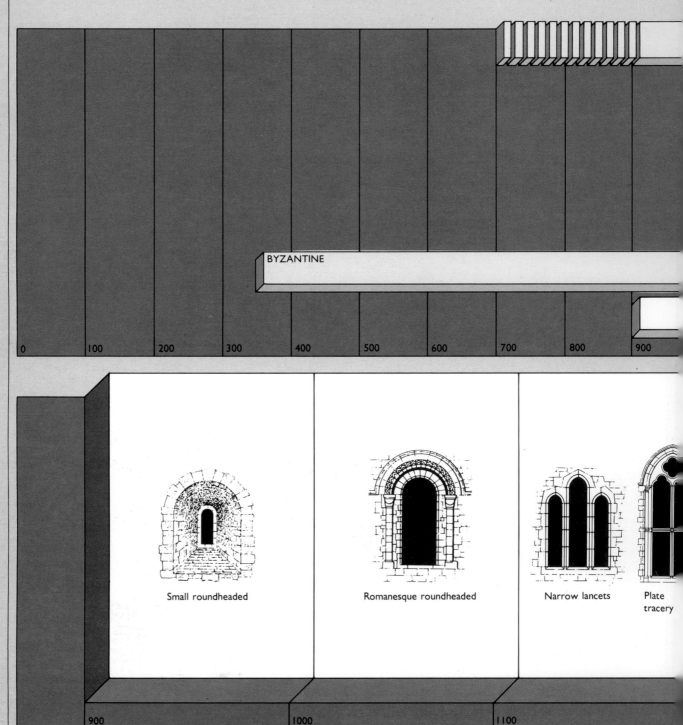

BYZANTINE

| 0 | 100 | 200 | 300 | 400 | 500 | 600 | 700 | 800 | 900 |

Small roundheaded

Romanesque roundheaded

Narrow lancets

Plate tracery

| 900 | 1000 | 1100 |

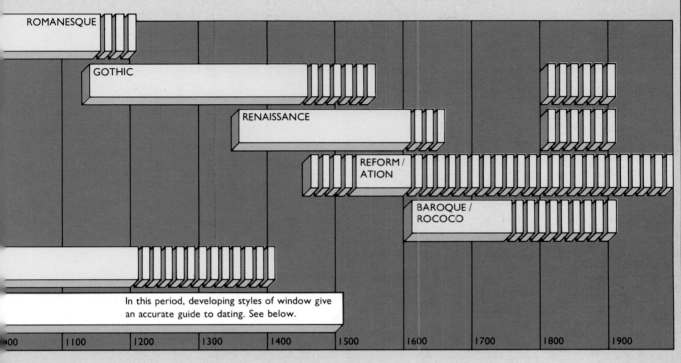

ROMANESQUE

GOTHIC

RENAISSANCE

REFORM / ATION

BAROQUE / ROCOCO

In this period, developing styles of window give
an accurate guide to dating. See below.

1100	1200	1300	1400	1500	1600	1700	1800	1900

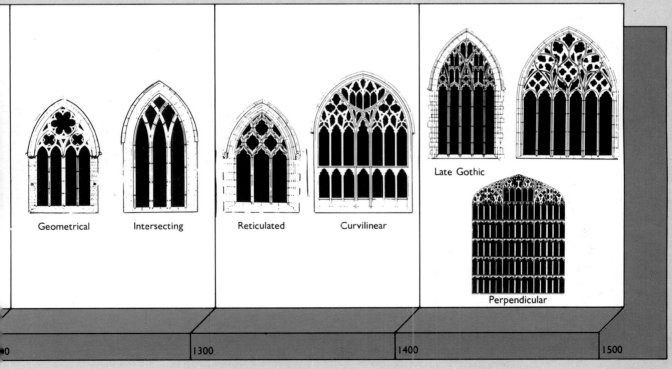

Geometrical   Intersecting

Reticulated   Curvilinear

Late Gothic

Perpendicular

1300	1400	1500

Arches and Vaults

THIS PAGE, RIGHT. *Sturdy, undecorated round-headed vaults in the crypt of Canterbury Cathedral.* OPPOSITE, LEFT *Gothic vaulting, decorated with delicate ribs and bosses.* RIGHT *Lace-like fan vaulting dates from the English 'Perpendicular' period.*

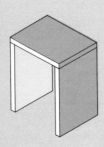

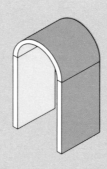

The problem of building doors and windows has been solved in a variety of ways. The structural strength of the building must not be lost because of these openings. The simplest solution is a flat stone or wood lintel which sits on top of the supporting columns.

After the Romanesque period rectangular windows were rare in churches. One reason was strength. The load on a lintel could easily crack it. An arch spreads the thrust and is inherently stronger. The natural strength of arches is such that they often remain in place after surrounding walls have collapsed.

A Romanesque arch is very similar to the arches used by the Romans in their vast building programme. Yet making round-headed arches on a large scale creates problems. The width of the archway is determined by the radius of the arch.

This causes particular problems where a narrow transept meets a wide nave: the different widths of arch have to meet at the same height and so the narrower transept arch has to begin its curvature higher than the nave arch.

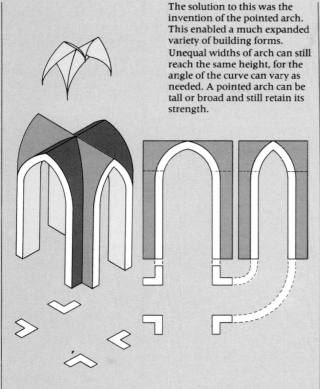

The solution to this was the invention of the pointed arch. This enabled a much expanded variety of building forms. Unequal widths of arch can still reach the same height, for the angle of the curve can vary as needed. A pointed arch can be tall or broad and still retain its strength.

The top of the arch can come within a few degrees of horizontal before it becomes weak. This style of flattened or depressed arch was very popular in the sixteenth century English style known as Perpendicular.

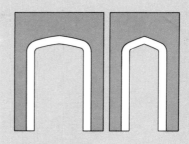

The principles of the arch are true of the vault as well. Vaults are simply a lattice of arches with some kind of infill between the ribs.

Vaults were a fashionable challenge to the architect and because of the expense incurred in their construction they were often built after the basic building was complete.

25

Fittings and Furnishings

By looking at some of the furnishings of the building we can see not only what it is used for, but also what sort of life and beliefs are expressed.

In many churches there has been a centuries-old tradition, dating back to the Old Testament of the Bible, to stress quality, artistry and craftsmanship: nothing but the best would do for the house of God.

This tended to shift the emphasis, however, from the church as people to the church as a building. So in 'Reformed' churches there was a return to a simpler style, emphasizing the building as a meeting-place rather than 'temple'.

Fonts

The font is used for baptizing people: the children or adults are sprinkled with water as a symbol of the washing away of their sin. In medieval churches the font was almost always positioned near the entrance to the church, symbolizing the entry into the family of God. In Baptist and some other free churches baptism is carried out by 'total immersion'. A baptismal pool at the front of the church is generally covered over when not in use.

ABOVE *An elaborate font cover.* BELOW *Designs drawn from pre-Christian Viking legends.*

Pulpits

The pulpit is the other main focal point: in churches and chapels emphasizing preaching it is often the main one. The teaching and preaching of the 'Word of God', the Bible, was re-instated at the time of the sixteenth-century Reformation, and the centrality of preaching is also reflected in other churches built at a time of revival and renewal.

When the new emphasis on

preaching led to the development of the galleried church, pulpits rose to great heights so the preacher could address the gallery as well as the floor level. Stairs led up to the pulpit, which in some instances was double or treble tiered – the lower levels used for announcement and readings, the uppermost level for preaching. The pulpit was normally placed against one side of the arcade.

Made just after the Reformation, this pulpit is built into the 'box' pews. Above is a sounding board or 'tester'.

Lecterns

The lectern often balances the pulpit on the other side of the nave. From here the service may be conducted, or at least the Bible 'lessons' read; but the preaching is from the pulpit.

Medieval brass pulpits are often in the form of an eagle, with spread wings supporting the Bible.

Choir Screens

Choir screens are often among the more ornate furnishings in the church. In Eastern Orthodox churches, the screens are covered with painted icons – images which are used to focus meditation and worship. By the end of the Middle Ages, with the stress on the 'priestly' function of the clergy and the mass as 'sacrifice' most churches were divided in two, the eastern end for the clergy and the west for the people. The choir screen marked the boundary, emphasizing the mystery of the service in the chancel. The screen had at least one door in the centre for processions to pass through, and was often surmounted by a **rood** – a crucifix attached to a horizontal beam. The choir screen is sometimes referred to as the rood screen. After the Reformation the choir screens were either removed or altered as a demonstration of the Reformers' teaching that all people could have direct access to God through Christ. There was no need for priests or sacrifice. In England the screens unfortunately became the most convenient place to put the organ pipes – in many churches the organ appears as an ungainly intrusion. Many screens were again built in the nineteenth century, with the revival of sacrificial ideas of Communion and the new interest in Gothic architecture.

Choir Stalls

The choir stalls are often the most impressive seating in a church. In monastic churches, the monks would use these tiered walled seats in saying their daily 'offices' – prayers and services said up to seven times a day. As this involved hours of standing in prayer, a narrow shelf-like ledge on the underside of a raised seat provided the monk with something to lean against. Called **misericords,** these props were customarily carved in a whimsical fashion.

In large churches elaborately carved seating was provided for the choir.

Tables/Altars

The communion table or 'altar' is often the focal point of the building. Where it is a simple wooden table this is a reminder of its use as a table for a memorial meal: at the Communion service it is used for the bread and the wine. A stone or marble altar may reflect a belief in the Communion or Mass as re-enactment of the sacrifice of Jesus (see previous section).

BELOW *In this church a modern communion table is placed closer to the congregation than the old one.*

Pews

Pews are today a dominant feature in many church buildings. It was not common to sit in church until the fifteenth century. At first the weary and laden had to bring their own chairs, but eventually the more far-sighted churches decided that it would be easier to provide seating. With the Reformation came the first regular appearance of pews is in Protestant churches, when preaching became the central component of the service. Seats were arranged in a semi-circle around the pulpit. Later they were fixed to the floor. By the eighteenth century pews were often 'sold' to families in the community. In some instances they were considered private property and decorated according to the owner's (sometimes peculiar) taste. In some churches there are box pews which date from this time, these were occasionally equipped with pádded armchairs and fireplaces!

Wooden pews, in this case 'box' pews, traditionally provide seating for the congregation. However, their arrangement is inflexible, so some churches now prefer chairs.

Memorial Tombs

Memorial tombs are a feature of many old church buildings. The early church's practice of burying the more famous or influential within the church building continued until the present century. The monuments, shrines and plaques in churches make an illuminating study in themselves. The various stages of church patronage can often be worked out. In some cases the monuments themselves came to be the church's most important asset.

Carved stone tombs and decorated 'brasses' mark the place where wealthy or prominent members of the community were buried.

Confessionals

Confessionals or confession boxes are common in most Roman Catholic churches. The priest sits to listen to those who make their confession. The box serves the purpose of focussing attention on the words of the priest rather than on his person. Confessionals usually have a small window or aperture to speak through.

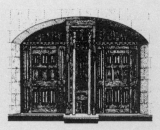

Candles

Candles begin to appear after about AD 1100. Gigantic candlesticks in some churches show the difficulty of trying to illuminate them by candlelight! Special lighters and snuffers soon followed.

PART 2
THE STORY OF CHURCH BUILDING

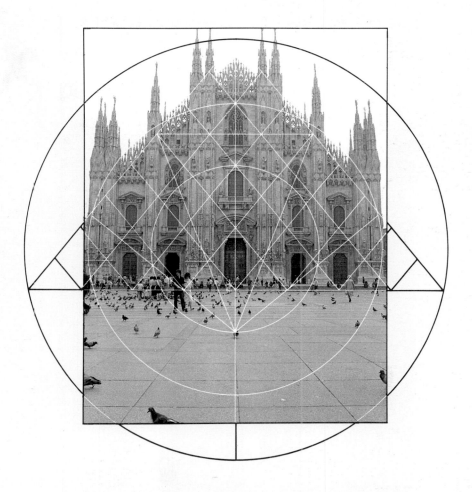

The last great medieval Gothic cathedral was built in Milan, Italy. Its entire construction was based on an elaborate geometrical grid of intersecting circles and equilateral triangles, which had a metaphysical meaning as well as a satisfying form.

The First Christians

In Jerusalem in the year 30AD, Jesus of Nazareth was crucified and his followers fled in despair. Three days later their lives had changed: Jesus had been raised to new life. As the weeks went by, they came to understand what this meant, and at last, Jesus left them for the final time. What were the disciples to do now? Jesus had told them that they were to go into all the world to spread the good news of new life – but first they were to wait for him to send them his Holy Spirit. Ten days later, on the feast of Pentecost, the Spirit came. This was the explosive birth of the Christian church.

As the first Christians were predominantly Jewish, the natural place to meet was the Temple or synagogue. The Temple in Jerusalem was an impressive building, the religious centre of Judaism, but it was not the right building for the new faith. The Christians believed that the daily ritual of sacrifice, the central part of Jewish ceremony, was no longer necessary. The death of Jesus on the cross was a once-for-all sacrifice for human sin.

A better 'model' for the Christian gatherings was the Jewish synagogue. The synagogue had been developed to maintain the Jewish faith when the Jews were in exile. By this time it had become the

Jerusalem was the spring-board of the Christian faith. In the first century it was dominated by the Temple, centre of the Jewish sacrificial system. In AD 70 this was destroyed by the Romans. The new Christians needed not a temple, for Jesus had died as a once-for-all sacrifice for sin, but a meeting-place. Their model was not the Temple but the Jewish synagogue.

meeting-place of the local community.

The tension between the idea of a church-building as 'temple', to re-enact the sacrifice of Jesus, or simply as 'meeting-place', has remained with the Christian churches since those early days. As the story unfolds, as we shall see, different groups have emphasized one side or the other, with profound implications for the style and architecture of the buildings they have used.

At the heart of the Christian faith is the belief that Christ's followers belong together. Early references to the Christians often mention their communal life and support. At first the common meeting-place was the home, and because the primary part of Christian worship was the celebration of the Lord's Supper, or Eucharist ('thanksgiving'), most of their meetings were held in the dining-room.

Houses in Palestine often had three or four stories and the dining-room was usually on the top floor (hence the 'upper room' described in the Gospels where the Last Supper took place). Christians would come together for an ordinary meal, probably prepared by the women of the group. Sitting around a large table on couches or benches the congregation would exchange news, study and pray together and review the work they were involved in. The supper would be concluded with a communal sharing of bread and wine in remembrance of Christ's death.

A meeting like this took place at Troas once, when the apostle Paul was the special guest. The book of Acts records how, during the long meeting in a crowded room, a young man perched on the windowsill literally dropped off!

Other meeting-places would be determined by circumstances or planning. Informal public meetings in the market-place might be organized for preaching. Meetings in the Temple precincts might be arranged to continue the dialogue with the Jews about who Jesus was. For a special visitor a large hall might be hired to accommodate the extra numbers, as when Paul spoke at Ephesus.

Small groups of Christians sprang up in the cities throughout Asia Minor and grew to become sizable communities. Because of the restrictions on domestic space, large churches often would be spread between homes. The first 'purpose-built' church buildings were generally similar to ordinary houses. Inside, the rooms equivalent to sleeping and living quarters would have been used as classrooms and for storing the

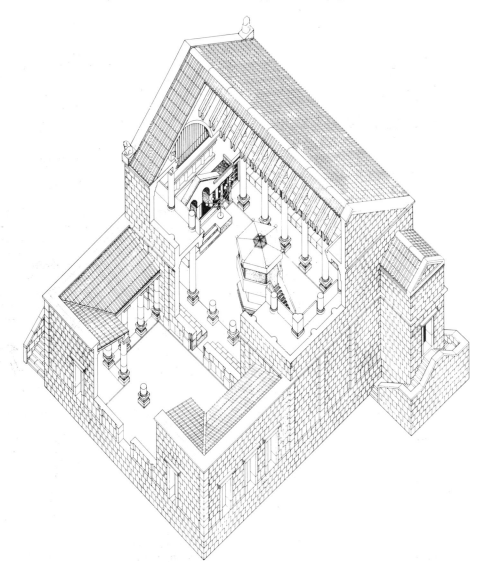

goods which were distributed to the poor. The large upper room would still have been the assembly areas.

The Christian population continued to swell in the second and third centuries. By the year 250 two-thirds of Asia Minor was Christian, and in Rome the community numbered between thirty and fifty thousand. Although the house-church would still have been an important place for worship, larger church buildings were constructed, patterned on the usual form for large halls, the basilica.

But building churches was not simple. Not only was there Roman red tape and crushing taxation, there was also constant uncertainty about the attitude of the Roman state to the church. The political wind could change overnight.

To begin with, the Roman Empire regarded the Christians as a Jewish sect.

They did not much care what people believed so long as they paid their taxes and treated officials with respect. But by the end of the first century the Eastern idea of ruler-worship had been imported to Rome. When it was applied as a test of loyalty to the regime, the Christians usually refused to venerate the emperor. Often this led to persecution and church property was confiscated or destroyed.

Yet the church continued to grow. Even the Roman persecutors were impressed with the Christians' fortitude in the face of torture and death. The tribulations may have dispersed the church, but far from destroying it, they toughened it. And as Christianity became more acceptable it attracted people in prominent positions, until eventually it was even adopted by its former enemy – the Roman Emperor.

The meeting-place for every Jewish community was the local synagogue. It was a simple hall with seats and a raised reading desk. Next to it there might be a room used as school or library.

The Official Church

The Emperor Constantine was converted to Christianity by a vision. He was instructed to put the sign of the cross on his soldiers' uniforms before a crucial battle. When the battle was won Constantine became the first powerful political leader to embrace Christianity.

Now, in the Edict of Milan in 313, the faith was recognized and granted official status. Though Constantine himself was not baptized until he was on his death-bed, he regarded himself as the thirteenth apostle, God's appointed 'vicar'. He asserted himself in church affairs by mediating in doctrinal disputes and presiding over church councils and he applied the leverage of the state to ensure that the decisions of those councils were upheld.

State patronage changed almost everything in the church. Simple house-groups gave way to larger congregations managed by full-time professional clergy. The participation of ordinary 'lay' people decreased, and ceremony became more pronounced in church services. Bishops and other church 'officials' took to wearing insignia of rank on their vestments in imitation of the status symbols of the imperial court.

These changes in the social profile of the church naturally affected church building. The domestic model was no longer adequate to accommodate the expanding needs of both clergy and congregation. One end of the church became the seat of the clergy, who were separated from the people by means of a screen and a raised floor. The simple wooden communion table was replaced by a more substantial and ornate one, becoming an altar, sometimes covered with precious metals and jewels.

Now that the dignity of the church was assured by imperial patronage, there was demand for buildings of the highest order. The model for these came from the architectural forms of public buildings – palaces, forums and temples. Yet it was clear to Christians that the pagan religious architecture of antiquity was not a suitable pattern. Temples in particular had unsavoury associations. Also the form was impractical, for temples were designed as a place for individuals to adore an image, not for large congregations to meet together.

So it was the official state architecture which was adopted. The most common form of public building was the basilica. In its simplest form this was a long timber-roofed hall ending in a semi-circular 'apse', with windows in the side walls. Such buildings could serve a variety of functions: audience hall, trading market, banquet hall, imperial forum.

Groups of Christians adapted the basilica to meet their own special needs or the wishes of a patron. Christianity was now socially acceptable, so there were funds enough for construction. Differences came from circumstances; a commemorative chapel sponsored by a wealthy patron would be more lavish and intimate than a basilica designed for a congregation of five thousand. Because there was no precedent for public church building, a great variety of experimental forms appeared.

Many small chapels were built as monuments to martyrs because of the growing veneration of those who had died under persecution. The 'martyria' often acquired porches, wings and rooms to accommodate those who wished to be buried near the martyr – almost as a superstitious way of guaranteeing salvation. Many of these memorials gradually became churches for the local community, and often required further rebuilding. This has been a common process: some Italian churches today are built on sites known to have been occupied by at least a dozen previous buildings.

Other churches were purpose-built to honour a saint or martyr and to accommodate a congregation. The old St Peter's basilica in Rome (replaced by the present building in the sixteenth century) was designed with a large 'transept' (or 'cross-piece') at the east end to permit pilgrims to circulate in front of the shrine. There was no seating. The service was conducted with the whole of the large congregation standing. Celebration of the Eucharist, the Mass, became a dramatic re-enactment of Christ's sacrifice: the action was now round the altar, and worshippers would be able to move around to view the pattern of service, the liturgy, more clearly.

By the end of the fifth century it was common to orientate churches so that as one faced the altar one was also facing east – toward Jerusalem. This became required

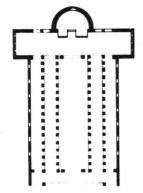

The style of building known as the basilica was common amongst wealthy Romans. Big basilicas were very suitable for larger Christian groups; there was plenty of space for the congregation and a natural focal point for ministers leading the service.

practice by the Middle Ages.

As the church consolidated its power, in Europe a more uniform architectural policy resulted. The nave and aisles of the early basilica developed into the classic form of the medieval cathedral. The pattern of service, the liturgy, influenced by the manners of the imperial court, was handed down to the medieval church.

The early alliance of the church and state clearly assisted the spread of Christianity. But the very expansion of the church's power brought difficulties with it. Some Christians were greatly alarmed by the

indentification with secular powers, particularly when emperors made decisions about church doctrine. The elevated position of secular rulers in the church hierarchy was intended to reflect the cooperation of a Christian society, but more often led to power struggles. The question of the nature of the church's authority in society was to become one of the recurring themes of medieval history.

THE BASILICA

The original form of the basilica was a long shoe-box-shaped building.

The interior of the building was generally brighter than secular basilicas and was often decorated with paintings of Christian symbols, geometric designs, words from the Bible and creeds.

②
The form of service (or 'liturgy') varied. The elders or clergy might be seated in front of the altar table or behind it. The bishop's throne or cathedra might be raised on a platform. An extension of this platform into the nave called an ambo would serve as a place for the reading of lessons.

The basilica of Santa Sabina in Rome is remarkably well preserved. It gives a good idea of the spacious interior, decorated simply with patterning on the marble surfaces.

①
The timber roof was supported by two internal rows of columns.

Secondary lowered roofs often covered the aisles and had windows above them onto the central nave.

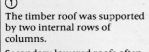
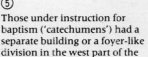

③
The eastern end of the building, where the service was conducted, was usually rounded into an apse.

⑤
Those under instruction for baptism ('catechumens') had a separate building or a foyer-like division in the west part of the church.

④
The side aisle and a clear space in front of the apse were used for processions, and so came to be known as the ambulatory.

The Eastern Church

Over the centuries the Eastern Church has developed separately from the West. In the Soviet Union the Russian Orthodox church is active (BELOW). In Greece there are tens of thousands of tiny chapels (OPPOSITE).

While the churches near Rome naturally developed the Roman style of building, the basilica, in the Eastern part of the Roman Empire rather different needs and emphases were developing. The great city on the Bosphorus, Constantinople (now Istanbul) became the centre of the Eastern Orthodox faith which continues its own traditions to this day.

The Eastern Church placed great stress on symbol and ritual. The clergy dominated the liturgy even more than in the West: services became priestly actions carried out on behalf of the people. The ritual celebration of the Eucharist was carried out in a 'chancel', a holy of holies separated from the gaze of the common people by screens.

The nave had become the place of the congregation in churches in the West: in the East the people were squeezed out still further, as the nave was used for processions and the congregation was relegated to the side aisles.

The solemn performance of the Eucharist in the East did not easily fit into the limits imposed by the basilica type of building. The basilica has no natural centre. A new type of building was required to accommodate the shift in doctrinal viewpoint.

One particularly well-known church reflects this new emphasis: Saint Sophia in Constantinople. Now an Islamic mosque, it was built by the Emperor Justinian in the early sixth century at staggering cost. Tradition has it that on the day of the church's consecration, referring to the Jewish Temple, Justinian exclaimed, 'Solomon, I have surpassed you!'

The centrality of the ritual was reflected in a central-plan building covered by a massive dome. The technical challenge required architects versed in structural dynamics, physics and mathematics. The dome had to be light enough to be carried by the walls, yet resilient enough to withstand the stresses of wind, weather and earthquake. Placing a dome on a square obviously limits the points of attachment, so it was necessary to design 'squinches' for the corners to distribute the weight evenly, so giving the interior of the building its characteristic octagonal shape.

The resulting building is enormous: full of mystery yet light and airy. Solid masses are made soft by tinted stone, cut and polished to show its patterned 'figure'. Silver, gold and acres of mosaics splinter the light from the windows in the rim of the dome and create a resonant sense of mystery. It is easy to imagine how the mystery of the building would have been heightened during its use. The congregation in the side aisles only catch glimpses of the processions. First comes the bishop in his robes, followed by the clergy bearing the bread and wine to the altar. Light from the dome falls in long rays in the mixture of

dust and the smoke of incense. The procession halts, then to the sound of bells and Greek chants slowly passes through the altar screen to the sanctuary beyond. The actual celebration of the Eucharist takes place out of sight in the screened-off chancel.

The rituals that were visible often were those reflecting the belief that the Emperor and the Patriarch were representatives of 'the halves of God'. Their ritual 'kiss of peace' under the great dome was a symbol of the religious and secular cooperation in the Christian state. This fusion of politics, theology and acting is difficult for us to grasp. For the man of the sixth century, the church building was a model of heaven on earth, a kind of preview of the presence of God in the company of the saints. The

clergy were the entrusted agents of communication with God. The radiance of the gilded dome of the church was a reminder to all in the city of the power of God and his representatives, and of the fact that God's ways can never be fully understood by men.

The mystical conception of Christian worship points toward the undefinable character of God's majesty. In the architecture of the Eastern church there is a pervading sense of those words the Bible uses to describe God - light, breath, and fire.

Often plain outside, Greek Orthodox churches are richly decorated inside – reflecting the fact that God is not simply concerned with external appearances. The atmosphere inside is also a reminder of the splendour and mystery of God. Often icons – images of saints – are used as an aid to worship.

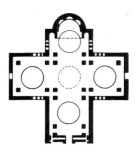

Many Eastern churches are built on the plan of the 'Greek cross', with four arms of equal length.

Commissioned by the Emperor Justinian as the greatest church of the Byzantine Empire, Santa Sophia in present-day Istanbul, Turkey, was the most ambitious building that had ever been undertaken. When the Turks took Constantinople in 1453 they turned it into a mosque, but even though they whitewashed over the mosaics and put up Islamic texts, the building still maintains much of its glory and mystery.

THE ART OF MOSAICS

Apart from the shape of the building, the most obvious innovation in the East was the splendour of the mosaics and other decoration. Some of the finest are to be seen in a city which lay on the border of the Eastern and Western Empires, the Aegean coast town of Ravenna in Italy.

Though the ground-plans in Ravenna are still mainly of the Roman basilica type, the decoration of the buildings from the fifth and sixth century is Eastern. Built for the imperial court when it had to remove from Rome in the fifth century because of barbarian invasions, most of the dozen buildings have been scarcely altered since their construction. In S. Apollinare Nuovo, for

instance, the lavish decoration transforms the piers and walls by an infusion of colour, making the large areas of stonework 'melt away'. There are horizontal bands of contrasting masonry, and the light filtering in illuminates the rich texture of the incised capitals and glittering mosaics.

The decorations are not just wallpaper. They reflect the meaning of the church and the history of God's acts of salvation. Kings, elders, prophets and saints are a reminder of the past and an aid to reflection and meditation.

This gold mosaic from the church of San Vitale in Ravenna is a portrait of the emperor Justinian who commissioned the building.

37

Christian Communities: the Monasteries

It was around the year 300 that groups of Christians in Egypt first set up communities 'away from the world' where they could live out in rigorous asceticism the demands of piety and self-denial. The remote monastery of St Catherine (OPPOSITE) at the foot of Mount Sinai was begun in the sixth century.

Other groups of monks live in greater contact with the outside world, in service and worship.

For all its splendour and status, the secularized church of Constantine's empire repelled some Christians because of its pomp and worldliness. Many of the dissatisfied joined monsteries – communities devoted to the disciplines of study, work and regular prayer. When barbarian invasions upset the secular foundations of the official church it was the monasteries which proved most hardy. Located in remote and often inhospitable places, the monasteries lived out the dark ages like seed pods awaiting a change in climate.

With Islamic invaders threatening Europe from the south and barbarian raiders attacking from the north, there were few places which afforded security. Many sought refuge in the desert. In the sixth and seventh centuries groups of monks left the Mediterranean by boat for the rugged coasts of Cornwall, Ireland or the Hebrides. Using dry stone-wall construction, the immigrant scholars built tiny fortress-like churches. Eventually these coastal monasteries so grew in size and strength that they sponsored missionaries to Britain, and took over the running of the Irish church from the bishops. The Irish church, perched on the edge of the known world, survived with vigour. For churches on the European continent, the climate was harsh until the ninth century when the migrations had slowed down and a greater political stability permitted the growth of monasticism.

The Italian monk Benedict was to become the most influential designer of patterns of monastic life. He upgraded the image of the monk and paved the way to the belief that gifts to monks were 'damnation-deductible'. As a result, land-owners, knights and princes liberally endowed the monasteries. They became formidable institutions. Eventually the rigours of vows became incompatible with the extravagence of financial management. The history of monasticism is a constant pendulum swing from reform to excess.

Contemplation, the disciplined attitude to work and (in most orders) access to books helped the monasteries develop the arts. The monastery of Cluny, founded in the tenth century, became for a time the artistic centre of Europe. It is not unreasonable to suppose that the architecture of the great abbey was the product of the minds of monks if not their hands. As Cluny grew in power and fostered satellite monasteries, its artisans and style spread too. Cluny supported pilgrimages and so its influence led to the construction of similarly-styled monasteries right along the pilgrim routes.

Monastery churches were commonly built in the form of basilicas with a number of transepts, often with towers. Because an active monastery would have over 400 monks, a great deal of space was required for them to say their daily offices, the seven set liturgies. If a monastic church did not also serve a local secular community, choir stalls might fill the entire nave – indeed some churches were constructed without naves. Theoretically, decoration was sparse. But St Bernard, the most famous of all medieval monks, had Cluny itself in mind when he asked other monks, 'Tell me, you professors of Poverty, what is gold doing in a holy place?'

The construction of monastic churches in remote locations taxed the skill and imagination of the builders. Built on mountain tops, into cliff faces or in the desolate emptiness of the wilderness, the structures posed immense logistical problems.

After the Reformation, the ascetic life lost much of its popularity and many monastic foundations were converted for other uses. New orders continued to be instituted until well into the nineteenth century, but the scale of monastic building never again equalled the scope of the eleventh and twelfth centuries.

Down the centuries, monasteries have been important centres of learning, teaching, medical work, missionary outreach and cultural life. Santo Domingo de Silos in Spain (RIGHT) dates from the eleventh century. Its peaceful cloisters are decorated with delicate sculpture of New Testament stories.

Foundations of Western Society: Romanesque

The development of the Romanesque style between about 1050 and 1200 has long puzzled historians. Buildings of this period all over Europe show a remarkable similarity – but no clear source. The term 'Romanesque' indicates the most obvious influence: late Roman building. Roman ruins abound in Europe today and there would have been many more in the eleventh century, but why would church builders suddenly begin to copy Roman architecture?

Close inspection of Romanesque architecture reveals many 'un-Roman' details - rugged 'chevron' ornament, fantastic carved figures and patterning which is almost like calligraphy. Scholars have traced some of these elements to Byzantine, Islamic and Celtic sources, an indication of the importance of medieval trade and pilgrimage routes.

One key factor leading to the upsurge of building in the eleventh century was the fact that the world had not ended! Christians believe that Christ will return to earth to bring this world to its conclusion. There had been a widespread belief that this

The five centuries following Rome's collapse in AD 476 gave rise to hardly any sizeable building in Europe except in the reign of the emperor Charlemagne. The chapel of his great palace at Aachen, Germany, (Aix-la-Chapelle) still stands. Octagonal in plan, it is built in Roman style.

In England, stone churches were built to replace former wooden buildings which have not survived. Windows were small (ABOVE), giving very sombre interiors (BELOW).

Even with their tall columns and more spacious interiors (OPPOSITE), churches of the Romanesque period were still dark. Extraordinary carving, for example at Souillac in France (INSERT), was common.

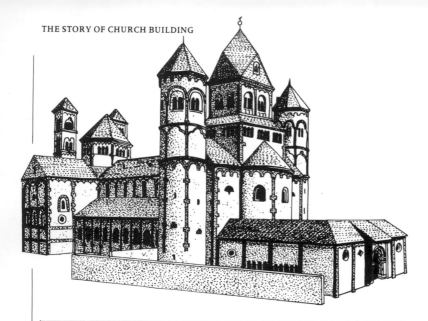

'Second Coming' would be in the year 1000. When Christ did not return, it was as if people waited for a while and then got back to work. By the mid-eleventh century a new enthusiasm for building had replaced the preparations for the Second Coming. Trade, commerce and pilgrimage blossomed. Cities sprang up along the busiest commercial thoroughfares. At the same time, new monasteries were set up along the trade routes. At first simple retreats, they became influential power-centres, wealthy enough to support lavish building programmes. Churches of hewn stone replaced wooden ones. They were larger, longer and more complex structures, many with timber or stone spires. Such churches would have been the most prominent buildings in the community, for virtually all domestic buildings were built of timber. So the local church was a matter of considerable civic pride. It was a landmark which could be seen from afar, and a cultural marvel to be examined at close range. On Sundays the whole town would meet there and a fair volume of trade would be conducted around it through the week.

Romanesque churches display a delightful variety of regional detail. In their basic structure and form, however, all are very similar. They are really modified basilicas. The main change was to the roof: timber roofs were replaced by tunnel vaults of massive masonry. Eventually the 'rib vault' – crossed semi-circular arches of stone spanning the nave – was developed. Stone ribs are stronger and more fire-resistant than timber, but far more complex to construct. Each stone had to be precisely cut. Timber forms called 'centering' held the stones in place until the mortar set. The spaces between the ribs were then filled in with a mixture of mortar and rubble on a woven lattice of willow branches. Later,

OPPOSITE *Romanesque churches in Germany are sturdy and solid, often with several towers. The monastery church of Maria Laach (*ABOVE*) and the cathedral at Speyer are typical. Inside, too, such as Mainz (*BELOW*), they are simple and dark.*

*Across Europe, styles and details were similar, whether in a French cathedral (Poitiers, *BELOW*) or an English parish church (Stewkley, *RIGHT*). English architecture of the period is known as Norman, since it was the Norman conquerors who brought it with them from France.*

vaults were built entirely from stone.

The extra weight of the ribbed vault and the stone walls of the nave meant that the arcade, aisle walls and buttressing had to be stronger. To the eleventh-century builder strength meant mass. Columns in Romanesque churches sometimes have the girth of a small elephant and walls often spread to fifteen feet thick. Round-headed arches linked the arcade to the aisle, and the windows echoed the shape. The weight, the simplicity of form and the logic of this system make these churches very attractive to us today (though to the Gothic architect they seemed 'childish'). The earliest Romanesque churches make up for any elegance they may lack by their great, solemn strength. The forms were extensively copied in the Romantic revival of the nineteenth century.

It was natural that changes occurred quickly in such an intensive period of building. The rough-and-ready masonry of the early Romanesque churches was soon replaced with more sophisticated work.

Later, columns were made of cylindrical blocks rather than stones laid like brick.

More complex elevations evolved. 'Blind arcading' emphasized the wall surfaces and linked the bays together.

Eventually the massive single column in the nave arcade gave way to the 'compound pier', a cluster of shafts bearing several different directions of thrust together at one strategic point.

The ground-plan of these churches anticipate the Gothic plans, with staggered apses, ambulatories and radiating chapels.

The nave bays are usually square in plan, and the aisles together take a quarter of the total width. These dimensions were determined by the restrictions of round arches. The outside of the church reflected the interior structure. Simple buttresses divided the side into bays and 'blind arcading' was the principle form of ornament.

One Romanesque invention was the twin western facade; an idea which was developed by the Gothic builders and has become the norm for church building ever since.

Perhaps the most notable legacy of the

Sweden has some delightful variants of Romanesque building at Vitaby (ABOVE) and Hagby (BELOW). Dalby (RIGHT) is the oldest stone church in the country.

Romanesque is its carving. Scenes on columns in the nave and cloisters were visual aids, with a dramatic scene around every corner. The artistic fashion of our own age makes us look at these rugged carvings as 'art' rather than as the lessons they were intended to be. Geometric carving was very popular, judging by the frequency of its appearance. Dog-tooth, chevron, ball-and-dagger, diaper, running dog – these are some of the names given to recurring designs; but many sculptors simply produced their own designs.

The riot of sculpture on the west front was intended to be an advertisement for the church and also a reminder of the seriousness of life. A common arrangement is that the major virtues and vices are portrayed on either side, with Christ on the Throne of Judgement between them. Considerable imagination goes into depicting the fate of the wicked. The society of the time was based on feudalism, with its underlying notions of obligation, duty, punishment and reward. So people readily believed that God 'kept score' just as they did. The sculpture on the front of the local church was an ever-present reminder of the

The doorway of Kilpeck church in the west of England (ABOVE) shows how local sculptors mingled Romanesque styles with local influences.

Churches on pilgrim routes in France are very large, with chapels around the apse so that pilgrims could see local relics.

The church of St Servatius in Maastricht, Holland, is built on the site of a sixth-century chapel. The Romanesque west end has been added to, over the centuries: the towers date from the nineteenth century.

Romanesque churches were built by itinerant craftsmen who took their designs with them. So there is an extraordinary similarity of style right across Europe. These three carvings showing Christ in glory come from church doorways in Moissac, France (RIGHT), Barfreston, England (ABOVE) and Soria, Spain (BELOW).

stakes of life, and of the need for the church, though the more basic Christian gospel of free forgiveness for the sinner was less clear.

The eleventh century marks the beginning of an all-embracing society. The church's authority and teaching extended beyond national boundaries. The solidity and imagination of Romanesque architecture reflects both the seriousness with which the church was viewed and also the magical world which medieval man saw all around him.

THE ART OF THE SCULPTOR

The earliest church buildings were quite plain. A community struggling to survive has little time for ornament and decoration. Image worship in surrounding pagan cultures also made some Christians strongly against religious sculpture at all.

As the church grew in size and power many members wanted to make the place of worship more prominent and more fitting. God is a God of beauty, they reasoned, and sculptural decoration can be used to express faith.

The use of sculpture in church architecture began to flourish in the Romanesque period. At first decoration consisted mainly of incised geometric patterns and floral ornaments, but the human figure (which has always attracted the artist) and other figurative sculpture followed. To illiterate people statuary and narrative scenes were a visual reminder of the serious truths of the Christian life.

Most of the Romanesque carving is not very naturalistic. By our standards their human forms are crude and stylized. But for the Romanesque artist and his patron these rough and ready figures rightly placed the emphasis of the carvings on the scene rather than the individual characters. Many of these carvings have an undeniable power, far in excess of smoother, more tastefully proportioned carvings from some later periods.

In Gothic art sculpture becomes more important in its own right. Figures are given a greater sense of weight and posture. They look at one another and gesture to the viewer with real feeling. The relationship between the sculptural groupings and the architecture as a whole also becomes more important. By the twelfth century sculpture was considered an essential part of a church and elaborate treatises were compiled about the proper arrangement of figures for each different part of the church.

Carvers working their way along the trade and pilgrim routes saw the work of other sculptors and engaged in a fruitful collaboration with other builders and masons. We know little of their actual working methods. There is some reference to the use of models, but the greatest emphasis seems to have been on theory. There were many attempts to discern underlying geometrical principles governing the human figure. Certain proportions were considered harmonious, and a vast lore of symbolic imagery was built up. Yet artists flexed these rules as much as they discussed them.

English sculpture in the Romanesque period was not as fine as French. Nonetheless, the work

In the fanciful details of many capitals and corbels we can see that the imaginative life of the sculptor was very rich.

Sculpture must have proved very popular, for in some churches it is hard to see the building for the decoration. In medieval English churches the west front is often wider than the building itself – making a

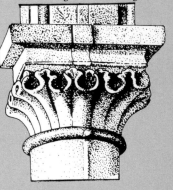

of some craftsmen was superb. This carving of six of the apostles is in the porch of Malmesbury Abbey.

kind of backdrop, much like that of the altar screen. This permitted a fuller display of statuary of biblical figures and saints (commonly painted in bright colours). In the cathedral at Wells, for example, the screen is so large that the doors scarcely rise above the level of the pediment. In France, by contrast, the doorways are much larger, with doorway arches often rising nearly to the full height of the church, and with many rows of statues carved into the moulding of the arch. The columns supporting the arch are often reserved for particularly notable figures – the archangel Michael or the apostle Peter standing guard with his set of keys.

The sculpture of west fronts is a study in itself. Romanesque churches tend to be covered with a writhing mass of people and mythical creatures with isolated clusters of the godly holding them at bay. The technical ability of the best of these carvings ranks them as important reference points for modern sculptors. Certainly the majestic pose of the 'kings' in the Chartres portal suggests an artist of sensitive humanity as well as commanding skill.

In modern churches taste and economics have severely curtailed the use of sculpture. There may be a few plaques or a small scene, but the modern world itself provides so much imagery through the media that sculptural portrayals have rather fallen into disfavour. Newer abstract experiments have not yet achieved the same universal language as sculpture did in the medieval world, and probably never will. Yet the attraction of carved things remains strong, and perhaps a greater use of sculpture in churches may be developed in the future.

Sculptors included charming detail in their work, even at points which are hardly visible to the human eye; this angel is from the cathedral at Rheims, France.

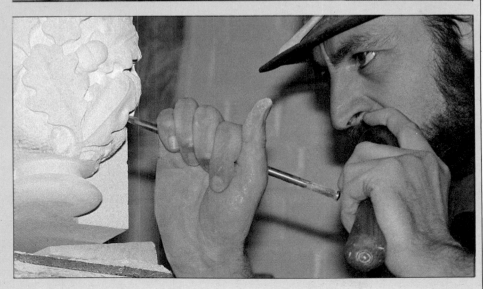

BELOW *Today sculptors are kept busy restoring old buildings.*

Pilgrims and Pilgrimage

Since the fourth century, the Holy Land has been a major destination for pilgrims. Sizeable churches have been built on the sites of Biblical events, for example the Church of the Nativity in Bethlehem.

The 'sites' of Christendom attract visitors by the tens of thousands today. Yet few modern tourists would think of spending two or three years on foot to reach their destination; fewer still would travel without money, maps or hotel reservations – all in the hope of ensuring salvation. But this was common in the eleventh and twelfth centuries.

It is hard to fathom the phenomenal magnetism the holy sites held. What we see is a host of churches which were important pilgrim sites, and a few seemingly superstitious objects which apparently made all the deprivation and hardship of pilgrimage worthwhile. The relics were of extraordinary importance. Without them there would have been no pilgrim routes, and probably no crusades either. Churches sprang up all along the pilgrimage roads, and it was those which had important relics which became the major stopping points.

There were three primary pilgrimage routes in the Middle Ages: to Jerusalem, to Rome and to Santiago de Compostella in Spain. Jerusalem was an important city for obvious reasons, for, as one early pilgrim wrote, what could be better than 'to put the finishing touch to virtue by adoring Christ in the very place where the gospel first shone forth from the cross'. Travellers could visit the Church of the Nativity, the Church of the Holy Sepulchre, see the place where Christ was put on trial before Pilate and revere countless relics. This was an

The long business of pilgrimage was for some an entertaining social event as well as a spiritual exercise.

expensive and time-consuming journey (up to seven years), made even more difficult since Palestine was occupied by the Moorish 'infidel'. Pilgrims to Jerusalem often travelled in armed bands; some of these journeys were little different from crusades.

Rome was important for two reasons. It was the seat of the Western church, and it was steeped in the history of the martyrs. It became customary for newly-appointed bishops to make the pilgrimage to Rome. A certain degree of confusion between ancient Roman statues and memorials to Christian martyrs added to the impression of the Christian heritage of the city. The most important relics of the pilgrimage to Rome were held in the Lateran Basilica; they were the heads of the apostles Peter and Paul. The church also exhibited the ark of the covenant, the tablets on which Moses wrote the ten commandments, the rod of Moses' brother Aaron, an urn of manna, John the Baptist's hair shirt, the five loaves and two fishes, and the dining table used at the Last Supper!

Despite this impressive catalogue, the most popular route was not to Rome, but to Spain, to Santiago de Compostella and the remains of the apostle James. At the peak of his popularity more than half-a-million pilgrims made the tiring trek over the Pyrenees to Santiago every year. They came primarily from France, but also from England, Germany, and Italy. Not all were devout volunteers seeking spiritual improvement. Many walked the road as punishment. Pilgrimage was prescribed as a means of penance. It was also a convenient way to banish trouble-makers; in thirteenth-century England, for example, the penalty for killing a relative was to go on pilgrimage in chains until they wore off!

The five major routes to Spain were dotted with churches, monasteries and hostels for the pilgrim. Among them are some of the most exquisite churches ever built. Vézelay on its commanding yet serene hilltop site was a marvel then and still is today. Poitiers, with one of the liveliest west fronts in France; Aulnay, with a carved portal showing the influence of Moorish artists, and Le Puy, where the whole church is somewhat Arabic; St Sernin at Toulouse with its immense interior . . . these are only a few. Thousands of architectural remains attest the vitality of the period, and any traveller in France will see them, restored, or in odd new uses: incorporated into the side of a barn or as a bicycle repair shop!

The major pilgrim churches all have a similar architectural form. All are spacious, with a long nave, aisles and gallery. All have wide transepts to hold the crowd of pilgrims and chapels to house the relics. The churches could get very crowded, particularly near the time of St James's day on 25 July. As a contemporary account said, 'No one among the countless thousands of people because of their very destiny could move a foot. No one could do anything but stand like a marble statue, stay benumbed, or, as a last resort, scream . . . The brethren, who were showing the tokens to the visitors . . . having no place to turn, escaped with the relics through the window.'

Some of the later pilgrim churches were designed with practicality in mind. The floor of Chartres cathedral is gently sloped and gutters round the walls allowed the floor to be washed after the crowds had left. The windows were designed to unlatch so that the building could be aired.

The pilgrim routes were important links in a primitive system of communications, and it is not surprising to find that they served as channels for architectural styles. French churches along the route to Spain show many Islamic details such as horseshoe arches and decorative arabesques, which came from Spain.

The tremendous flurry of building along the pilgrim routes in the twelfth century gradually subsided. Festivities and commerce began to obscure any spiritual goals. The Renaissance and the Reformation then undermined the pilgrim spirit. But pilgrimages continued until well into the eighteenth century.

Perhaps the most striking observation to make today is that the art and architecture of the period was thoroughly integrated. The sculpture of the portals, capitals and screens was part of an all-embracing scheme aimed to encourage and teach the traveller. There are different styles and different artistic treatments sometimes drawing on local folklore, but they all tell the same stories. The artist and architect were in no doubt about what their work should communicate.

Tombs of martyrs have been popular pilgrim sites. At Canterbury, pilgrims visited the shrine of Thomas à Becket who was assassinated in 1170 after refusing to allow the state to limit the church's action.

The church of Sainte Foy at Conques in south-west France is typical of churches on the pilgrimage routes to Santiago de Compostella in Spain.

RELICS

The lists of relics are both fascinating and macabre: Peter's tooth, the blood of Jesus, a piece of the head of John the Baptist, bones of Mary Magdalen, a finger of the apostle Thomas, a phial of Mary's milk . . . and all of these were part of one church's collection!

The natural liking for souvenirs and superstition are two of the reasons behind the medieval fascination with religious relics. Originally intended as an aid to devotion, the relics soon seem to have been worshipped in their own right. They were traded, collected, taken on tour. People took oaths on them, and built churches over them.

RIGHT *Relics were often stored in ornate cases which themselves became the object of veneration.*

BELOW *St Ambrose was the influential adviser of Emperor Theodosius in the fourth century. After his death his body was put in a specially-built basilica in Milan, where he had been bishop.*

It was Helena, mother of the Emperor Constantine, who first actually hunted for relics. Visiting the Holy Land in 326 at the age of sixty-nine she unearthed what she believed to be Christ's cross. This she shipped back to Constantinople. From there over the years it was disseminated in splinters as gifts to the worthy.

By the eleventh century overt worship of relics was commonplace. The church taught that the martyr's example of sacrifice should be followed by the faithful, and therefore took great stock in relics as visual aids. The crusades swelled the number of these mementos in currency.

There is no doubt that virtually all of these relics were spurious – either intentional swindles or innocent mistakes. Cynics have speculated that there are enough relics of 'the true cross' to construct the Spanish Armada! But notions of 'truth' in the Middle Ages were vastly different from our own bias for empirical 'proof'. The relics were considered 'true' because they had the power to aid worship, even to bring healing, and above all to provide an emotional insurance policy.

They were certainly powerful. The relic bones of St Foy were acquired by the monastery of Conques in France by outright theft. A monk infiltrated the neighbouring monastery at Agen and waited ten years for his chance to make off with them in the night. Conques quickly shot to prominence and Agen folded.

Such was the worth of relics that complex procedures were devised to safeguard them. Workmen excavating the site of a monastery in Reading, England, found a mummified hand built into the old foundations – surely the monastery's prized hand of St James, hidden before the building was destroyed. As the church's most important asset, relics were prominently placed in the building. The small chapels off the apse which were so common in the twelfth century were built to display reliquaries. Caskets were fashioned in gold, silver, enamel and jewels to house the remnants, often with small glass windows through which the object could be revered. These caskets themselves were fitted with handled carrying cases so that they could be taken on ceremonial processions.

Artists were hired to paint pictures of the relics, usually surrounded by scenes from the life of the saint. These paintings themselves commonly became objects of veneration in their own right. Martin Luther, for example (before he began to question such practices), hired Lucas Cranach the Elder to paint some of the 9,000 relics in the collection of the local archbishop as a kind of medieval promotional brochure.

By the early sixteenth century the mania for relics had subsided. The confident humanism of the Renaissance dispelled much of the general fear and insecurity of life and death. The Reformation attacked relics as flagrant idolatry; the violent rampages associated with the Reformation destroyed many of the prominent relics, as well as statues and church furnishings.

THE CRUSADES

Some crusaders marched out of genuine trust that it was 'the will of God' to liberate the Holy Land from the Muslims. But there were other factors. The prospect of winning new lands, coupled with the promise of religious merit, had a great appeal.

There were four major crusades. The first in 1097, reasonably well organized and highly motivated, managed to capture a number of key cities, including Jerusalem. But subsequent crusades foundered for lack of enthusiasm, funds, and above all, strategists. At last the fourth crusade, detoured from its original plan in an effort to pay its transport debts to the city of Venice, attacked the capital of the Eastern Church, Constantinople. Thus one of the more bizarre architectural effects of the crusades was the dispersal of the spoils of Constantinople.

RIGHT *During their occupation of the Holy Land, the crusaders built churches at important sites. The church of St Anne, Jerusalem, is a beautifully preserved example of crusader architecture.*

BELOW *The crusaders took arms to oust the 'infidel' from holy sites.*

The Viking Craftsmen: Stave Churches

Some of the most intriguing churches ever built grace the rugged Norwegian woodlands. Built in the eleventh to thirteenth centuries, these all-wooden buildings are called 'stave churches' because the timbers used in their construction are like the staves of a barrel.

They are among the earliest churches built in Norway. Christianity came to the region through the Vikings' contact with Christians in England and Ireland. The churches built by these returning sailors are clearly inspired by their familiarity with ship-building. Shipwrights techniques were used throughout; a keel beam ran down the centre of the roof; there were trusses, elbow joints and brackets virtually the same as those of a Viking longboat.

Stave churches were constructed on a sub-frame of massive hewn and notched tree trunks, raised off the ground by boulders. Great masts were mortised into these beams to support the stacked roofs. Working with axe, auger, plane and chisel (saws were an expensive rarity), Norse builders fitted the walls into slots in the beams and locked the joints with well-seasoned wooden nails. The close tolerances they achieved are attested by the fact that, after centuries of storms, some of the churches still stand – their joints still tight.

One unusual feature was an outer 'ambulatory' right round the building. This provided a porch where the people could stamp off the snow – and deposit their weapons! It also helped to protect the foundations of the church.

The interior of the church was dim. A few small windows high in the walls were augmented by candles; many of the initial 800 churches must have collapsed in flames. The chancel was built as an annexe and decorated with large hanging tapestries. Some interiors were painted, but the real decorative forte was wood carving. The writhing, interlocking patterns of the carvings combine the mythical beasts of Norse legends with Christian symbols. The predominant theme of the exterior carving is the adventures of the Norse hero Sigurd. Like others in Norse mythology, he is eternally condemned to endure the effects of his mistakes. These pagan narratives may have been a kind of ready-made local 'Old Testament' for the Norwegians – a prefiguring of Jesus.

The Viking trade routes led to a fertile artistic exchange: the style of the carving is very like Celtic work. It is also possible that the small wooden 'stock' churches of Ireland provided inspiration to the builders of stave churches.

Some of the most delightful decoration occurs in the only metal-work in the building – the doorlock. Iron was painstakingly gathered from the bottom of bogs where sediment from decaying upstream deposits had settled. It was smelted in a highly romantic and difficult procedure and shaped with hammer, tongs and anvil to a finish which would impress the most demanding smith.

Viking converts to Christianity merged some of their old beliefs into their new faith. The dragon-heads on the shingle roofs of stave-churches are ancient Viking symbols. This church is at Vik in Norway.

THE ART OF THE CARPENTER

Wood has always been an attractive building material. In some climates well-chosen timber can last almost indefinitely. The stave churches of Scandinavia are a delightful example of both the solidity and warmth of totally wooden structures.

Stone buildings require the use of wood as well, and the carpenter was an essential member of the master builder's army. In the medieval period the master builder himself was expected to be a proficient woodworker.

Timber was usually felled while the foundations for the church were under construction. The trees were chocked up off the ground and left to lie for six months or a year. This seasoning made the timber more stable when cut, and also lightened the load to be transported.

The two most favoured woods were oak and pine, the former for structural work and the latter for scaffolding, centering forms for arches and ceilings, windlasses and general purposes. At the building site timber would be cleft or sawn to rough shape and then prepared with adze and planes. Drawings were made on the shop floor and the carpenter worked with ruler and dividers to transfer these measurements to his work.

Almost all the work was done prior to installing the piece in place. Large beams were awkward to manoeuvre, so there was no point in 'trial and error' fitting. Completed components were numbered and stored until they were needed. For a major construction such as the internal bracing for a tower or steeple, this meant that the carpenter had to have a grasp of the whole construction as well as the parts. During construction pieces would be hoisted up in order and secured with wooden 'tree nails' or trunnels. The holes for these pegs were precisely misaligned so that as the peg was driven in it would pull the joint tight.

The carpenter was also required to make the ladders and scaffolding for the masons. Some of these were ingeniously designed modules which could be easily dismantled and reassembled. During construction of the walls the masons left square holes in the stone work at regular intervals. The scaffolding fitted into these and was held fast by means of wedges.

When the walls were in place, the carpenter could begin assembly of his most important contribution – the roof. The construction of a roof was planned to ensure that the outward thrust against the

BELOW LEFT *Tree trunks would be roughly cut to shape where the tree had been felled.* RIGHT *The finished article, such as this bench end, would not be carved until the wood was fully seasoned.*

supporting walls was kept to a minimum. This meant that the roof had to be extensively cross-braced. Each brace had to be fitted to its respective rafters and tie beams. Today these units would be assembled on the ground and then hoisted into position by means of a crane. For the medieval builder it had to be done piece by piece. Obviously the joints had to be made with great precision or the roof would not fit together. It was exhausting and dangerous work.

When the basic structure was complete and the building was watertight the carpenter could begin on the furnishings. There were doors to be made and hung, choir screens to be designed, carved and fitted, and a variety of smaller woodworking tasks. Here the carpenter had the opportunity to show his skills in carving and joinery. Oak was the preferred timber. A large choir screen or reredos (the backing screen over an altar) would again be made in hundreds of pieces and pegged together. The carpenter knew how to position the grain to facilitate carving and cutting mouldings, yet maintain strength. As most churches were unheated the wood tended not to warp or split (until heating was installed in modern times!).

The delicacy of some of this work draws admiration from even the most skilled woodworkers today. The work is infused with a spirit of dedication and good humour. The carpenter may or may not have seen his work as a service to the glory of God, but he clearly felt that only the best was good enough. There is little sign that he used inferior short cuts. In our machine age tools have brought speed and accuracy to woodworking, but these techniques have also bred a dependence on the machines. As a result many of the traditional skills of the carpenter are now near extinction.

Wood was vital both for structural work, such as roof vaults, and for the furnishing of the church, such as the choir screen.

An elaborate choir screen (BELOW) is made from hundreds of parts pegged together. This beautiful pulpit, in contrast, is carved from a single tree trunk!

In New Zealand, wood was plentiful when the cathedral in Auckland was first built; the structure could also resist earthquakes.

The Power and the Glory: Gothic

Grandeur and majesty are the key notes of the church of St Denis in Paris (OPPOSITE). *The influential patron wanted the building to express the majesty of God. The result set the style for the whole Gothic style of building.*
The 150-foot-high nave of Europe's largest cathedral at Cologne (RIGHT) *and the filigree spire of Freiburg cathedral express this same emphasis, pointing upwards to God.*

No programme of building in history expresses the conviction and common faith of a people as does the building of churches during the Gothic era. The statistics are astounding. During the twelfth and thirteenth centuries more stone was quarried in France than had been used in ancient Egypt. Foundations for church buildings dropped thirty feet, often with a mass as great as the building above. Spires soared to the height of a forty-storey skyscraper (Strasbourg cathedral) – often the result of plain competitiveness between builders. Amiens cathedral was so vast that the entire population of the city (10,000) could attend at once. Beauvais was built so tall that a fourteen-storey block of flats could fit inside. Winchester cathedral is 556 feet long – enough to fit one and a half football pitches in it.

In France from 1050 to 1350 over 500 large churches were built and tens of thousands of parish churches covered the countryside. There was a church or chapel for every 200 people, a ratio which has never been surpassed. The importance of the church in every sphere of human activity was paramount.

The cause for this dynamic period of building inventiveness cannot easily be isolated. The spread of monastic orders and their organizing influence certainly helped, as did the growth of the pilgrimage routes. By the early eleventh century cities were growing fast, and as the development of civilization is always allied with urban life, it is possible that the intellectual life of the cities spawned the new style.

But if causes are unclear, timing certainly is not. There are few watersheds in architectural history which can be pinpointed as accurately as the Gothic. The style originated in the east end of the Parisian church of St Denis. It was here that a powerful and ambitious church leader by the name of Abbot Suger sought to remodel his church in keeping with the religious thought of the day. A fifth-century Greek theologian called Dionysius was one of the prime contributors to twelfth-century thinking. (At the time he was confused with

Rich materials and textures inside medieval churches added to the majesty of the buildings. This silver chalice comes from Sweden.

a third-century Dionysius, the patron of Paris, and also with a Dionysius who was a contemporary of Paul!) His writings emphasized mystical enlightenment and stressed that the church should be patterned on the heirarchy (he perceived) in heaven. Numerology, the symbolic interpretation of numbers, figured prominently in his work and had already been influential in Byzantine worship. Other Greek philosophers were also read avidly, and their concepts of the 'divine proportions of the universe' seemed to have obvious implications for the building of churches.

Suger and his contemporaries sought to apply this mixture of Greek and Christian thinking to the requirements of the church. Suger also courted the patronage of the royalty and guided the king in the role of the 'apostle of France'. (Secular rulers commonly claimed divine authority, some even termed themselves 'vicars of Christ'.)

The buildings display a more sophisticated knowledge of structural dynamics than is evident in Romanesque work. In particular, the new pointed arches work 'differently' from the old rounded ones. But this feature in itself is not what makes the new style.

What is different is something less tangible – a sense of order, of lightness in materials and lightness in illumination. Suger and his mastercraftsmen seemed to make the new choir in St Denis (St Dionysius) defy gravity. Gone are the ponderous piers and massive internal buttressing. The walls are thin, the windows large. The ambulatory and radiating chapels are not just mortared together but flow in a harmonious rhythm of pointed arches and slender shafts. All the components have been considered together. Suger was a keen collector and believed that the beauty of God could only be understood through the effect of beautiful things on the senses – quite a radical idea in the Middle Ages!

The effect on kings, peasants and churchmen must have been stunning. Here was a building which transported the visitor in a kind of mystical levitation. It was rational, elegant and mysterious, full of light and opulently decorated.

Suger's builders achieved this effect by some subtle means. The buttresses on the outside of the choir are carefully positioned to be as invisible as possible from inside.

A unique drawing of the west front of Strasbourg cathedral shows something of the craftsmanship that went into every part of the great Gothic churches. A comparison of the plan with the result (RIGHT) shows very few differences.

Pointed arches permit flexibility in the placing of the piers. By carefully positioning supports to receive stress, the architect could use tall thin piers in the place of the ponderous columns of the Romanesque. The result is a space with the three features which were to become the hallmarks of the Gothic style; verticality, achieved through height and visual stress on vertical lines; lightness, created by large windows and slender buttressing; and unity, with all the architectural details integrated into one whole.

The Gothic style quickly spread through western Europe. Itinerant architects carried it to England, Germany, Italy and Spain. There is even a 'French' Gothic cathedral in Upsalla, Sweden. The style changed in

Twin spires are common. The church at Deventer in Holland (ABOVE LEFT) *and the great Gothic cathedral at Uppsala in Sweden both have simple and striking spires.*

Even small village churches had grand towers. English churches (BELOW) *are often decorated with crenellated tops.*

OPPOSITE *The late Gothic ('Perpendicular') college chapel of King's College, Cambridge. Universities were originally guilds of students attached to cathedrals. The college chapels of Oxford and Cambridge have no naves: like the chapels of other communities no space was required for a congregation.*

Thousands of churches were built in France. Even the most out of the way were often superb buildings. This one, for example, is complete with rose windows and flying buttresses.

contact with local traditions and taste. Where the French had sought great height in the nave, the English produced naves of monumental length. The Italians preferred extensive use of arcading on the exterior, and the Germans became masters of the tower and spire. Though 'high gothic' was primarily a French invention, the many regional interpretations co-mingled. And all shared the same symbolic interpretation.

The burst of building in the twelfth and thirteenth centuries has left lasting monuments not only to the ingenuity and sensitivity of those charged with construction, but also to the elaborate attention given to the clergy. The layman could not participate in the services. It was thought that God was too holy to be approached by untrained people. So the people merely watched the rituals conducted on their behalf.

Because of their education and the authority of church offices, the clergy became a powerful class. Though their role was to be servants of God, the all-too-human temptations of power caused problems. By the late Middle Ages the elite position of the clergy was becoming excessive – and so, too, was their wealth. One particular excess was the sale of ' spiritual privileges'. Wealthy families would pay large sums to have mass said for them and their deceased relatives in chapels within the church. Charges were also levied for the viewing of relics, for blessings and for special masses. The proliferation of ritual and magic did neither the clergy nor the layman much good. When the authority of the Pope at the top of the pyramid was questioned, tremors were felt right down to the local parish. The great age of Gothic building was only possible because of a total belief in the security and authority of the church. The church in ' Gothic times was relatively more powerful and influential than government is in our age. There was no shortage of wealthy patrons to finance church building – and there was a considerable degree of competition which also fired the efforts of builders and patrons.

Attempts to revive the Gothic style in the nineteenth century produced many buildings with a superficial resemblance to the great Gothic cathedrals. But the similarity was only superficial. The understanding of the church, of the world, of God's requirements of men had changed in the intervening centuries.

The term 'gothic' was first used in the seventeenth century. Goth-ic meant 'like the uncultured Goths'. It was not meant to be complimentary. 'The external appearance of an old cathedral cannot but be displeasing to the eye of every man who has any idea of propriety and proportion,' says Tobias Smollett in 'Humphry Clinker' (1770). 'Natural imbecility,' complained Sir Henry Wotton in his 'Elements of Architecture'. 'It ought to be exiled from judicious eyes.' Another critic termed Gothic architecture a 'congestion of dark, monkish piles without any just proportion, use or beauty'. Needless to say that negative verdict has been reversed today.

CHARTRES CATHEDRAL

The cathedral of Chartres has been extravagantly praised as the most splendid architectural space in the world. Anyone who has spent a sunny day in its garden of coloured glass and soaring stone stems would probably agree.

In the twelfth century Chartres was a respected intellectual centre, with a monastery, universities, libraries and churches. It had connections with royalty and was essentially a twin capital with Paris. Churches had occupied the town's hilltop site since the eighth century. Though Chartres was not directly on the pilgrimage route, it was itself an object of pilgrimage. The church possessed a highly venerated relic, the tunic of the Virgin Mary. Worship of Mary, rare in the early church, had become very popular by the twelfth century (almost all the major French Gothic cathedrals are dedicated to her) and Chartres considered itself specially favoured in being protected by the Virgin.

In 1194 the old cathedral burnt down. All that remained were the western towers. While the building was still in flames the dean of the cathedral found an architect to undertake the rebuilding. Work started the same year. The dean and the other church officials volunteered three years of their own substantial salaries (the dean's salary alone would have been equivalent to £250,000/ $450,000 a year!). Further financing was assured when the Virgin's tunic was discovered unharmed in the rubble-filled crypt. The enthusiasm of the building project is virtually impossible for us to understand: our civilization has no comparable 'centre'. Townsfolk from far and wide brought building materials and provisions. A semi-permanent town-within-a-town was erected to cater for the builders.

Everyone agreed that the new structure was to be far more glorious than the old. Indeed many believed that the Virgin had willed the fire, in order to clear space for a more impressive edifice. But the architectural problems were immense. The existing Romanesque foundations were strong, but the walls were very far apart for a roof as high as the one proposed. The solution was daring. The upper reaches of the nave walls were pierced and lightened by huge windows, and the outward thrust of the roof was supported by a system recently developed in Paris – the flying buttress. The result was in interior space larger, lighter and brighter than any other of the time.

Inside, the architect simplified the nave by eliminating the tribune gallery, which traditionally had been used as a kind of balcony for worshippers. There was liturgical reason for this departure. As the celebration of the Mass had become increasingly important, so a great emphasis had been placed on the viewing of the bread and wine – the 'elements'. Many contemporary accounts tell of worshippers having visions of Christ at the instant when the bread and wine were held aloft. It must be remembered that these were thought to be the actual presence of Christ himself. Doing away with the gallery meant that the whole congregation was united in the nave at this key moment in the service. The simpler nave design also created a greater sense of spatial unity in the sanctuary. This solution was subsequently copied in all the classic cathedrals of France.

The riches of Chartres' decoration are virtually inexhaustible. There are more than 10,000 figures in the

With its weathered copper roof and twin spires, the north one built three hundred years after the simpler south one, the cathedral dominates the town.

Serene figures of kings guard the Royal Portal – the great west door.

sculpture and stained glass. Some scholars have spent more than fifteen years studying the themes in the building! The pictures and story cycles are not merely ornamentation: they are a recitation of the basics of Christian belief applied to every area of life. In an age when few people could read, the building itself told stories. The decoration was an attempt to embody all man's knowledge of the world, and to tell the story of God's action in history. There was a sense that any further learning could only be a refinement of what was already known.

The visible church building was both a symbol and a model for the invisible or 'spiritual' church. The cruciform shape of the church represents both the cross, with the altar as 'head', and the four points of the compass, signifying the extended community of all believers. The church was considered to be a tangible expression of a host of images and ideas expressed in the Bible. It was the body of Christ, a city of refuge, the New Jerusalem, God's presence among men. Some people carried this symbolism to every detail of the building and saw the roof tiles as soldiers of Christ and the steps to the altar as the apostles.

Most of this complex allegory would have been lost on the layman. Indeed even with binoculars it is difficult to make out the figures in the clerestory windows. No matter. Just as the learned theologians could always understand more, so too the cathedral embodied more analogy, allegory and moral symbolism than could ever be grapsed by one person. The very richness of its composition was a symbol for the wealth of God's grace.

The tall columns of the nave reach up elegantly. On the left is the triforium of the south transept.

THE ART OF STAINED GLASS

Glass is as old as the Egyptians, though the glazed window was not developed until Roman times. Cast glass has been found built into the walls of the ruined cities of Pompeii and Herculaneum. Glazed windows were particularly valued in the colder northern climates, but curiously until the tenth century most European glass was imported from Greece. The art of stained glass manufacture began in earnest in the twelfth century.

Coloured glass was produced by adding various metallic oxides (gold, copper, cobalt, manganese and so on) to a molten mixture of sand and potash. (The red produced by this process was of such intensity that it had to be laminated to clear glass so as not to be too dark.) When the right consistency had been achieved, the glass was blown into a cylinder, and unfolded to make a 'sheet'.

The construction of a thirty or forty-foot window was a time consuming craft. This was

French artist Gabriel Loire puts the final leading into a window which shows the story of Noah.

especially true of the early twelfth century windows, when the average size of the fragments was less than two square inches! First the glazier would whitewash a long bench. On this was drawn the placement of the iron bars to support the window. (The joints between lead and glass are very fragile and a large window would collapse from its own weight if it were not wired to this support.)

The design would then be drawn and glass cut to fit. Glass was cut by slowly drawing the tip of a hot iron over the glass – a method which produces a high percentage of rejects. Doubtless these scraps were incorporated into other designs.

When all the glass was cut for a particular part of a design the glazier would then paint the glass with a mixture of iron oxide and a low-melt glaze. The purpose of the painting was not only to treat details too small for glass and lead, but also to control the flow of light through each part of the window. When we look at a bright light in a dark place, we see around it a kind of 'halo' which makes it seem a good deal larger than it really is. So in a stained-glass window the light from each piece of glass tends to 'etch' into the opaque line of the lead strip around it. The glazier often painted the edge of the glass darker where it met the lead to soften the

contrast so that the brightness of each fragment could be controlled. This is an astonishing feat. The unfired glaze looks nothing like it will after the glass has been refired in order to fuse the 'paint' to the surface. The glazier could never really know what a window would look like until it was finished and installed. Working with a small team he proceeded from figure to figure, drawing and copying, squinting and imagining.

The stained glass of the twelfth and thirteenth centuries has rarely been equalled in quality and beauty. The crude manufacturing process produced glass with imperfections which greatly enhance the quality of light. These early windows have a mosaic-like evenness and the jewel-like fragments splinter the light into a rich texture. Later glass, though technically 'better', is often artistically worse, for two reasons. First, improved fabrication produced glass which was uniform in quality – and quite characterless. Second, artists tried to copy the fast-growing techniques of painting. They spent lifetimes trying to reproduce in stained glass effects which can really work only on canvas. The results are rarely as pleasing as the simple mosaics of earlier windows.

If the style of medieval windows was simple, the content was certainly not. They often show complex allegories. A common variety is the 'type–antitype' where an image on the left side of the window is 'explained' by another on the right. The 'Good Samaritan' window from the cathedral of Sens in France is a good example. (It is also interesting because two identical windows were made. The second was originally at Canterbury. There was a fruitful exchange of ideas between English and French glaziers in the twelfth and thirteenth centuries.) The man 'going down from Jerusalem' is compared to Adam leaving

Architects today make use of stained glass to create a particular mood. This is the lantern of the Catholic cathedral in Liverpool, England.

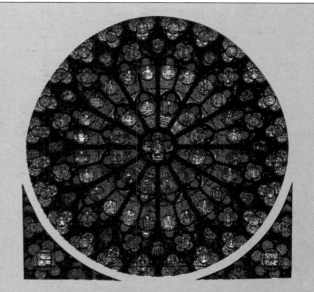

Paradise. He is fallen upon by thieves (the seven deadly sins). The priest and the Levite (the Old Testament Law) pass by and at last the poor man is cared for by the good Samaritan (Christ).

Such riddles were very common. One can almost imagine an earnest prelate explaining the significance of a metaphor to the bemused glazier, tongs in hand. Saints were also popular subject-matter. In the reknowned 'tradesmen's windows' at Chartres each of the windows donated by a guild advertises both their craft and their patron saint.

In the late thirteenth century another type of window was developed, the 'grissaille'. This was predominantly white glass cut in small diamond-shaped panes and decorated with small sections of colour. This had the advantage of letting more light into the church. Indeed a nave illuminated by old glass could be so dark as to make reading impossible on a dull day.

Stained glass windows have

The great south rose window of Notre Dame in Paris, 42 feet/14 metres across, is a collection of Bible stories in glass.

had their enemies. After the Reformation thousands were shattered. In the eighteenth century the English architect Wyatt removed the old glass from Salisbury cathedral to make the nave lighter. He sold the lead for scrap and used the glass to make drainage for the cathedral precincts! Nineteenth-century 'restorers' often made copies of the old windows which to our eyes look characteristically 'nineteenth-century'. Bombs during the two World Wars blew many fine old windows apart. Today the greatest enemy is probably pollution; the old glass is gradually wearing away, eaten by the acidity of the air.

The Church Builders

The great churches and cathedrals were built by professionals. The architect or master mason was familiar with all the various skills which went into the construction of a building. He asked a substantial fee, and got it. Travelling with a team of trusted workers he supervised every aspect of the work. Groups of masons even organized conferences to discuss building techniques – attracting masons from many countries. Each mason had his own drawings and cloth rolls containing essential measurements, angles, and means of calculating stress, which were his reference book. He often actually owned quarries.

After drawings were accepted by the patron, the first task was to organize delivery of materials. Anyone building in the twentieth century knows how difficult and aggravating this job can be; it used to be worse. Until the nineteenth century it was common to transport building materials by ox-cart and barge; the former meant that roads had to be built and the latter not uncommonly meant diverting rivers! River transport was preferred because of cost and load capacity. Stone would sometimes be finish-cut in the quarry and given a mark to indicate its final position in the building. Another mark would show who had cut it, since the workers were paid per block.

Supplies were often given to building projects, but this generosity could be subject to abuse. One benefactor gave a bishop permission to cut 'as much timber as his men could remove in four days and nights'. Imagine his fury when the bishop brought 'an innumerable troop' and denuded a large part of his forest!

Facilities set up on site would include a host of stone-cutters' workshops, kilns for burning lime to make mortar, saw pits for cutting timber, forges for making metalwork, other kilns for glaziers and store houses for materials and tools. The basic tools of the stone-cutter were mallets, bow drills and chisels. Perhaps the most interesting tools were those used for measuring and 'machines' for lifting heavy

Lifting materials into place was one of the difficulties the builders face. Elaborate machinery was designed to do the job.

weights. Measuring tools were simple, but in expert hands could produce work to extremely fine tolerances. To find a right angle for reference the builder would lay out a triangle with sides three, four and five units long; the two shorter sides joined at 90°. The architect could check the accuracy of the strings stretched out for foundations, and other angles could be derived from the right angle. Two sets of footing walls were built, one to carry the arcades and the other to support the exterior buttresses.

After the foundations had set and settled (a year or two) the first courses of stone would be laid at the east end of the building. Mirrors and water-filled wooden troughs were used to check horizontal levels, and plumb-lines to check the verticals. Working from east to west the builders would first raise the internal arcade and then the walls and buttressing. To lift the cut stones into place a variety of windlasses were used, often large man-powered 'squirrel cages' with a rope wound round one shaft. Smaller loads of stone and mortar were carried with hods or wooden buckets. Scaffolding was usually erected by leaving holes in the walls where horizontal beams could be inserted and roped to vertical supports.

The construction of vaults required experience. First the shape of the ribs would be drawn on a 'tracing floor' – a large white-washed or plaster-covered floor. Templates were made from these drawings so that the cutting of the stone could be checked continually. A wooden centering form was then built to the inside dimensions of the arch and this was secured to a movable scaffolding under the first bay to be vaulted. The stones were laid along the centering from alternate sides until at last the keystone was put in place. When both ribs were in place the centering would be moved to the next bay and so on down the nave. Additional forms were used to support the infill between the ribs – though in some churches this is only rubble, straw and plaster.

The main difficulty in the construction of church towers was the problem of height. Scaffolding had to be constructed on site, so that heavy components could be brought up in stages. But the difficulties did not deter the craftsmen from showing real care.

Few large churches or cathedrals were built in a generation. Most were constructed over centuries, with later styles superimposed on the earlier. In some places, such as the transept of Winchester

Cathedral, evidence of the improvement in construction technique during the period of building can be seen; the later joints are thinner and the surfaces more precisely worked. Standards for measurement might also change. At one time in England the basic unit was the rod, which was determined by marking out the length of sixteen grown men's feet! A later mason might very well arrive with another standard – for there was no efficient co-ordination of measurement until well into the seventeenth century.

Because of the time such a building required to construct, it was generally put to use for services well before completion. A temporary wooden 'west end' closed the building off, and oil-soaked linen filled the window spaces. The sound of chisels, the creak of wooden gears and the shuffle of feet on boards high overhead must have made a curious accompaniment to the chanting of the mass. One can understand the great ceremonies which attended the consecration of each completed section of the building.

THE ART OF THE BUILDERS AND MASONS

Many do-it-yourself enthusiasts have worked with wood at some time or other, but few have attempted to cut stone. The specialist stone-cutters today rely on tools such as diamond-edged power-saws, pneumatic chisels and high-speed engraving tools, and use protective goggles. To cut flowing organic forms from stone with a mallet and chisels thus seems even more of a feat.

Just as it is easier to carve lime wood than ash, so too each type of stone has its own 'grain' and other characteristics. Certain types of stone have always been pre-ferred for carving ornate capitals; others are better for constructing walls. The master builder therefore had to have a good eye for stone. He had to evaluate the qualities of local stone, and work out the quantities required.

The first job at the quarry was to free large chunks of rock so that it could be cut into the required shapes. This was done in several ways. Holes were drilled into the stone during the winter and filled with water. When the water froze it would expand, splitting the rock. Another method was to light fires which would heat the rock and then to cool the rock suddenly by pouring water on it to make it split.

Once the boulders had been freed the masons could go to

work. The master builder would supply the dimensions, and each mason would have his own ruler, square, and calipers. Lines would be drawn on the surface with chalk. Chisels with coarsely serrated edges were used to rough out the work. Final shaping and polishing were sometimes accomplished by rubbing the stones on another hard flat stone. Most of the basic build-ing stones would be cut and shaped in the quarry and given the mark of the workman (workmen were generally paid per stone). These dressed stones are called ashlar.

Pieces destined to become capitals or moulded sections were usually transported to the mason's lodge at the building site. Here there was a drawing floor covered with chalk or plaster. Using a combination of flat drawings and wooden templates, the master carver made the more complex com-ponents. Important carvings such as capitals and statues were roughed out in the lodge and then installed before finishing. This eliminated the risk of damaging fragile under-cuttings during installation.

Stone carving is very laborious, and bits which break off cannot easily be 'glued' on. The master carver needed to be a patient sort, but efficient and fast. In addition he needed to be sensitive to the wishes of the patron and aware of the latest stylistic developments. The secrets of the craft were carefully guarded among the masons.

The next time you look at stone carving try to imagine what it would be like to carve some of those intricate shapes. Imagine the steady tapping of

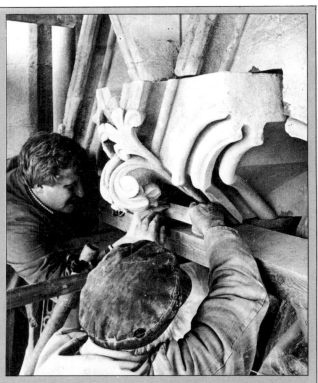

the mallet, the flying chips of stone, the dust and the constant measuring. Try to envisage the atmosphere of the workshop, the stories, the comments made by other stone cutters, the long hours and the cold feet. It was hard work, a labour which placed an emphasis on time and accomplishment which it is difficult for us to understand today.

A piece of stone is precisely cut to size and carved.

The Ascent of Man: the Renaissance

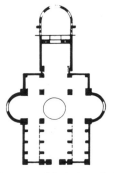

Renaissance architects drew their inspiration from classical forms. Church plans were far more compact than Gothic ones.

Commissioned by Pope Julius II in the early 1500s, the monumental new St Peter's in Rome (OPPOSITE) was worked on by all the famous architects of the time. The result was a triumphal statement of the institutional church's power and the builders' genius.

BELOW *The sculpted gold doors of the great Florence baptistry. Portrayals of biblical scenes were now not 'other worldly' but lifelike.*

The Italian architect Alberti was a prototype of what was to become in the late Renaissance the ideal man. He built churches and public buildings; he was an accomplished horesman and athlete; he studied law, physics and mathematics; he painted, wrote plays, poems, music and a treatise on economy, and was renowned for his dazzling wit.

Alberti and the other great architects of the Renaissance – Bramante, Raphael and Michelangelo – enjoyed a new type of artistic prestige. Rather than being skilled tradesmen building churches for the needs of the Christian community, they were artists, expressing their insights. Fifteenth-century Italy was quite prepared to acknowledge earthly as well as heavenly brilliance. Even before the Renaissance the architect had been highly regarded, but now the artist's vision was regarded as sacred. And over the centuries, this shift from tradesman to visionary has had a profound affect on the role of the artist.

A dramatic change in ideas about man in the fifteenth and early sixteenth century brought about a revision of cultural, political, economic and church life. The new thinking began in Florence, spread throughout Italy and then followed the trade routes north.

Already in the late Gothic period the combination of Greek thought with Christian concepts had gradually focussed thinking men's attention on the nature of man himself. Art of the time shows this. Portrayals of Christ began to stress his human nature, for example; representation of saints were less concerned with symbolism and more with anatomy. In all walks of life, the nobility of man was becoming the key theme. In Italy this humanism grew with the development of a merchant class. Independent traders and bankers seemed to fare quite well without an unduly subservient attitude to the church. New commentaries on Greek philosophy emphasized the nobility of man and the individual's need to take his potential into his own hands. Artists became more highly regarded, too, and found a new source of patronage in the merchants to supplement their reliance on the church.

The church, of course, was still a powerful institution. Indeed, the Renaissance popes readily adopted the manners and pretensions of secular rulers. In the cultivated self-awareness of the age, they sought to modernize the church in keeping with their own confidence.

Church building was often sponsored by princes and merchants as well as the clergy, so the requirements of services were not usually the main concern. This can be seen simply by looking at the ground plans of most Renaissance churches. The chancel is smaller, the crossing larger. The dome over the crossing has become the true focus of the church. The scale of the buildings has also changed radically. The soaring height of a Gothic nave made a person feel dwarfed, humble and contrite. Now the Renaissance churches are scaled to a more 'human' level.

The vertical stress of the High Gothic has been replaced by a careful balance of proportions. The mystical space of a Gothic church is gone, and the tangible mass of walls and sculpture have once more been emphasized. For example, the standard arrangement of side aisles is altered by making each bay a separate chapel, slowing down the speed at which the eye can 'take in' the building.

In the Middle Ages it was generally acknowledged that construction of a church took more than a lifetime. Like an ancient tree, a cathedral would sprout new branches from generation to generation. But the Renaissance was concerned with wholeness, and so it was unthinkable that a church should be altered after it had been built. When Pope Pius II had a cathedral built in his home town of Pienza he decreed that no one should ever add or remove anything, or even alter the colour scheme of the interior.

The church architecture of the Renaissance is rather like entries in a competition, with each new building trying to be more perfectly proportioned and detailed than the last. New methods of construction were developed, and there was an excited dialogue among the architects and intellectuals. But the life of the church does not always move at the same pace as the building. The same ideas which produced Renaissance churches eroded the faith that the buildings were supposed to serve.

Back to Basics: the Reformation

By the late fifteenth century the church knew it was in trouble. Laxity and corruption was wide-spread amongst the clergy and authorities seemed deaf to the pleading for a crackdown to save the church. Rome dragged its feet. Running the ecclesiastical bureaucracy was costly and reforms would certainly reduce revenue.

While the church dithered Europe exploded. Movements of protest and reform had already prepared people for the inevitable revolt against a corrupt and oppressive system. Renaissance learning and a new class of literate activists questioned both the doctrine and policy of the church. The development of cheap printing encouraged people to read, compare and draw their own conclusions. By 1500 over 30,000 titles were in circulation in Europe – most of them religious works. So when Martin Luther in Germany publicly protested against the practice of 'selling tickets to heaven' to raise money for St Peter's Church in Rome, there were plenty of others to support him. The issue of course went deeper. Can we earn our way to heaven by good works, or is it, as Luther discovered for himself in the New Testament, a matter of trusting in God's grace alone?

Changes to churches after the Reformation show dramatically how beliefs are expressed in church buildings. Zwingh's church at Zürich, Switzerland is typical of churches throughout Protestant Europe: the altar for the celebration of the mass, high in the chancel was removed; seats were put in its place. The focus was now the pulpit half-way down the nave.

Luther in Germany, Calvin in Geneva, Zwingli in Zurich thrashed out the theology of the issues. The response from the church authorities was defensive. Popular support was enormous: the new message was a liberating one.

But one response to the teaching of Luther and the other reformers' was a wave of idol-smashing iconoclasm. The reformers rejected many traditional church practices: confession, pilgrimage, relics, prayers for the dead, clerical celibacy and ecclesiastical wealth. These had no foundation in the Bible and undermined the gospel of faith in Jesus Christ as being all that is necessary to approach God. Rowdy crowds tore down monasteries, smashed statues and stained glass – and displayed none of the virtues of spiritual enlightenment. The reformers tried to restrain them, but the church was an easy target, rich and soft.

'Protestantism', as it was to be called, took hold. By the mid-sixteenth century Western Europe was firmly divided between Catholics and Protestants. The Catholic church did eventually institute far-reaching reforms, but the breach was too wide to be closed.

It was one thing to throw bricks through stained-glass windows and quite another to develop alternatives to the medieval pattern of worship. The kernel of Reformation thought was that people could not enter into a relationship with God, or grow in that relationship, without hearing the gospel preached. The focus of worship shifted from the ritual re-enactment of Christ's death at the altar to the preaching of God's word from the pulpit. The cavernous old churches, well suited to creating a sense of mystery, were acoustically dreadful for preaching. This became even worse after the removal of the rejected choir-screens, icons and altars which symbolized the separation of priest from people.

How could the building, then, be made to suit the people's needs? The reformers did not eliminate the communion table, but gave it a position of less prominence. The pulpit was moved into the nave, generally attached to one of the pillars. A large sounding-board behind it helped combat echo. The sermon became a fixed part of the service, and so benches were provided for the congregation to sit in a semi-circle beneath the pulpit. Sometimes an additional reading desk or lecturn was built on the opposite side of the nave. The whole idea of what the communion service meant

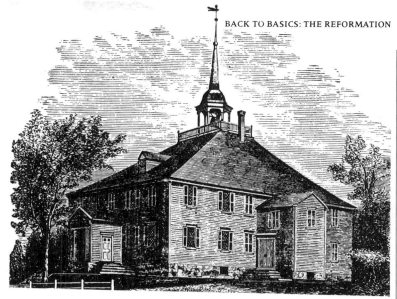

changed. The reformers considered that it was not a re-enactment of Christ's sacrifice, but a celebration of what that sacrifice meant. The people were now to take part in it. In some churches, the table was moved from the position of 'altar' at the east end of the church down to the chancel steps. Simple wooden tables were used instead of stone altars.

Chantry chapels, no longer used to say mass for the deceased, were sometimes converted to libraries or teaching rooms or used for wedding services. The multi-coloured medieval wall paintings were painted out.

The resulting space was cool, bright and large. The seventeeth-century Dutch painter Pieter Saenredam gives us a good idea what Dutch Reformed churches looked like in the 1600s. The nave remained open through the week and was a popular meeting place.

The austerity of the all-white interior was softened by the gradual accumulation of monuments, plaques with creeds and the like. But the biggest introduction was generally the organ.

The early stages of Protestantism did not require new church buildings; the

Protestants took over the existing church buildings and adapted them for their own use. But as old buildings fell into disrepair and as congregations grew, new facilities for worship were required. The new buildings reflected the doctrinal shift from altar to pulpit. There was much experimentation with the shape of the church in an effort to permit the preacher to use a normal speaking voice. 'L' form, 'T' form, cross,

The Pilgrim Fathers were radical Protestants who sought a new start, away from repressive European state churches. This church built in 1686 shows how their building style reflected their 'clean sweep' attitude.

St Andrew's, Holborn Circus (LEFT) was one of the churches Sir Christopher Wren built in London after the Great Fire of 1666. With its gallery, dominant organ and pulpit and classical style it is an elegant expression of formalized post-Reformation protestantism.

BELOW *The artist Pieter Saenredam recorded what Dutch churches looked like in the seventeenth century when they had been cleared out after the Reformation.*

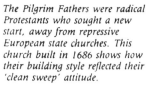

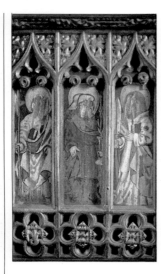

The Reformation had its destructive side. All over Europe, beautiful carvings were defaced and stained glass smashed as people revolted against medieval abuses.

A meeting of Quakers (RIGHT) typifies the radical Reformation groups. Most, such as the Anabaptists, stressed the sole authority of the Bible without the need for church hierarchies. They were the forerunners of Baptist churches today: Congregational and other churches also date from these 'gathered churches' which stressed the 'priesthood of all believers'.

round, oval, polygon – virtually everything was tried. They all attempted to concentrate on the principle liturgical centres of pulpit, communion table and font.

Later, a major innovation was the introduction of the gallery, which made it possible to fit a larger congregation into a smaller space. The English architect, Wren, even conducted experiments to determine the maximum permissible distance from the pulpit in all directions before 'clarity' was lost. Hearing the preacher became the main consideration in church design. With the advent of galleries, pulpits grew taller to reach up to them. In the Frauenkirche in Dresden (1738) there were five tiered galleries and the pulpit was at the second-storey level! Many free church buildings still used today are built with galleries, no chancel, but impressive positions for preacher and organ.

In the New World, architects had a clean slate. America in the seventeenth and eighteenth centuries was full of architectural experiment. Traditional English church styles were reinterpreted in the most abundant local material – wood. The Anglicans (Episcopalians) tended to build rather nostalgic imitations of medieval English parish churches, complete

with carved chancel screens. Puritan building, on the other hand, tried half-a-dozen different liturgical arrangements, all of which stressed the position of the pulpit. The form of the parish church devised by Wren and Gibbs became rooted in America in the nineteenth century, and produced some of the most attractive 'post colonial' buildings.

The Reformation could not instantaneously produce its own architecture. By trial and error it settled on a variety of 'hall-church' types. Reformed churches tend to emphasize clarity, order and solemnity, features which can produce elegant architecture, but can also be quite plain and boring. The desire to make these church interiors more 'spiritual' was one of the key motivations behind the nineteenth century revival of 'ancient styles'.

LEFT The reformers realized that through new hymns with popular music, it would be possible to 'sing the Reformation into the hearts of the people.' The organ soon became an important feature in churches.

The Drama of Religion: Baroque

The style known as Baroque was both new and a continuation of the elaborate sculptural building of the High Renaissance. It received impetus from several sources.

The Protestant Reformation (which coincided with the High Renaissance) presented a frightening challenge to the Roman church. At the Council of Trent in the mid-sixteenth century the Catholic church set about putting its house in order. Reforms in church doctrine and practice were easier now because by the time of the Council virtually all the dissenters had left. The founding of the missionary and teaching order, the Society of Jesus (the Jesuits) was part of the same aim – to reunite the church under the papacy. The restored authority was used to organize the church both administratively and liturgically, and as a result of these efforts the Catholic church regained many areas lost to the Protestants in the Reformation. By the seventeenth century national boundaries, governments and religions were more clearly defined than ever before. Northern Germany, Scandinavia, the Netherlands and England remained predominantly Protestant. France was Catholic but less dependent on the papacy than Italy, Spain and Portugal.

The Baroque style developed most quickly in these southern areas, but was not limited to them. Neither was it purely a Catholic style – though later it was thought to be so. The missionary excursions to Central and South America in the eighteenth century helped fortify the Roman church and the Baroque style soon took root there, blending with the local forms of decoration to produce churches of astonishing complexity.

The early Baroque churches in Italy are characterized by a sense of drama and mystical religious feelings. The cool experiments of the Renaissance yield to the urge for more emotional experience. Catholic theology placed great importance on the mass as a dramatic re-enactment of Christ's death, on savouring the mysteries of the gospel and on feeling the wounds of Christ suffered on one's behalf. As a result, everything about the churches has emotional and symbolic meaning. Through

The church at Wies in Bavaria is a lavish example of the Baroque style. The almost overwhelming ornamentation is designed to exalt the worshipper, emphasising the drama and mystery of religion.

Details such as sculpture (BELOW) and metalwork all contributed to the overall effect.

The Baroque style began in Italy. The church of Sant'Ignazio in Rome (CENTRE) *dates from the 1690s. Its extraordinary ceiling was designed to appear like the gate of heaven itself.*

the lavish texture of the interior the worshipper is to be caught up into the realm of the infinite. Led by the senses, he is intended to transcend them.

In essence Baroque church architecture returns to the medieval spirit. But the means used are quite different. The medieval cathedral focussed on the sacramental elements; the Baroque church was an all-encompassing totality. The skills of orchestrating sensual experience, refined in the Renaissance, were put to full use in the Baroque.

The church buildings were metaphors for the gates of heaven itself. In many churches this is almost literally true. The ceiling is a painted illusion of the heavens; the whole roof of the building dissolves into the glorious realms above. Theatrical means are employed throughout the building, and these relate to the events taking place over the altar – the ascension of the Virgin, St Michael and the Dragon or the vision of a saint. These churches work like cinema: they have plot, sustained drama and conclusion. Ingeniously placed windows spotlight the dramatic groups.

Compared to the writhing interiors, Baroque exteriors are relatively plain.

The style of European Baroque churches, such as the church of Vierzehnheiligen in South Germany (LEFT) *was taken by Jesuit missionaries to other parts of the world, such as Mexico* (RIGHT).

Straight lines are often modulated with curves and the sheer bulk of the church is emphasized. The Baroque churches of South America are an exception in that they are rarely plain, and when there is abundant ornament it is richly coloured.

The magnificent church of Vierzehnheiligen ('The Fourteen Saints') in Northern Bavaria, Germany, is a good example of late Baroque at its most sophisticated. The west front is calm and stately. The interior is so complex that it is impossible to 'understand' it without referring to a ground plan. In fact the nave is comprised of four interlocking ovals, with circular transept arms. The oval plan became popular in the second half of the seventeenth century and seems to epitomize the builders' urge to make the church a symbol of the union of heaven and earth.

The refinement of the Baroque style, lighter and less frenzied, is known as Rococo. Rococo ornamentation is more abstract and 'frothy' than the Baroque, and less obviously theatrical. By the late eighteenth century several other stylistic currents were blending with the Baroque and Rococo. In particular, the world of ancient Greece and Rome was once again a key influence.

The Baroque church is an exuberant chorus of sensory experience designed to foster spiritual vision. This direct effect on the senses has proved to have a continuing appeal; indeed there are few Baroque churches which are not still in use today, and Baroque forms of decoration still sell well in our machine age.

Every part of the building was richly decorated. This door is from a church in Spain.

THE EXPORTED CHURCH

People take their beliefs with them when they travel. European commerce in the sixteenth and seventeenth centuries opened trade routes to Asia, Africa and the New World.

The most vigorous exporters of the church were the Jesuits who combined trade with missions in South America, India and the Philippines. They supervised church construction and trained locals in building techniques. Invariably their churches have a pronounceed regional style. The elaborate Mexican churches, for instance, owe as much to the local Indian style of convoluted carving as they do to the Spanish Baroque tradition.

Missionaries had a difficult decision: should they 'christianize' the local religious architecture, or should they import Western forms which would be free of misleading associations with the old religions? They usually chose the latter. Today the balance has shifted. New churches often follow local forms.

The cultural cross-currents of the exported church have generated many mixed styles – but also some beautiful buildings.

Many churches in 'mission areas', such as this chapel in Fiji, were built in imitation of traditional European styles. Today there is greater emphasis on reflecting local styles and culture.

In the eighteenth century Central America was an important missionary area.

Missionaries taking their faith to other cultures have realized that there is nothing particularly sacred about their own forms of worship, let alone buildings. This simple meeting place is in East Malaysia.

The Birth of the Modern Age

In the mid-eighteenth century the established church was in decline. Science and philosophy were growing fast, and the idea of Progress captured the minds of the people as religion had done in earlier ages. The brash new philosophers not only attacked the bureaucracy of religion but even dared to question the existence of God.

What began as an intellectual ferment soon became a revolutionary political action. The American Revolution delivered a blow to the old order. Then the Enlightenment, born in the drawing room of aristocratic French idealists, became a revolution which shook the foundations of Europe. The Industrial Revolution, though not overtly religious or political, ensured that the old order would never return. In France, part of the violence was directed against the established church. Many beautiful buildings including St Denis and Cluny were badly damaged, and it was proposed that Chartres should be pulled down and replaced with a 'temple of wisdom'.

Yet curiously this turbulent century was also a period of religious revival. In America, England, the Netherlands and Germany itinerant preachers revitalized churches. The Moravians and Methodists particularly had a strong missionary outlook. Preaching in the open air, tents, houses or wherever they could, they brought a spirit of conviction to their testimony of God's love. Waves of revival swept the Protestant nations.

One result was that scores of churches

were built by new groups of Christians. It is hardly surprising that the building was sporadic and stylistically varied. By and large, the Rococo style was rejected as being unsuitably frivolous. The simple functional style was Neo-classic, yet another return to the source of Roman antiquity. Neo-classicism differed from earlier classical revivals in being both more consistent and more austere. New revelations about classical styles came through excavations of the Roman town of Pompeii and caught the imagination of architects and people alike.

By this time the position of the professional architect had been firmly established and architectural practices had been set up. The Roman styles were carefully analyzed and measured drawings of columns, capitals and pediments were

American churches of the eighteenth century (LEFT) *have a simple, graceful style. The layout, with no lower side aisles, is known as a 'hall church', reflecting the hall-type meeting-places of the radical Reformation.*

In England, the aristocracy sometimes built churches in their own estates. This private church shows the influence of Italian architecture.

Forwards or Backwards? The Nineteenth Century

In 1800 most of western Europe was dominated politically by Napoleon's France and intellectually by the ideals of the Enlightenment. Science, industry and philosophy appeared to be making great strides and there was a romantic optimism about the future of mankind, an optimism which was decidedly secular.

This hope for a bright future coupled with a new interest in the order and beauty of Greek culture gave birth to an architectural style called Romantic Classicism. Arcades of Ionic columns sprang up on public buildings, shopping arcades and church façades. Until this time, Christians had rejected the Greek temple as an architectural model because of its pagan associations. But this was no barrier to the nineteenth-century designers who saw in the temple not paganism but order.

The interest in classical antiquity was matched by an enthusiasm for the Middle Ages. In both France and England there was revived interest in Catholic liturgy. The Anglo-Catholic movement of nineteenth-century England was a conscious effort to recapture the mystery, beauty and intensity of worship. An idealized view of medieval life led to conscious attempts to imitate Romanesque and Gothic buildings. These styles seemed to have an inherent 'spiritual' quality about them, a quality which more and more people were beginning to miss in the new 'machine age'. By mid-century it was becoming apparent that the 'triumph of reason' was making much of the social fabric quite unreasonable. Devout revivalists hoped to provide an alternative by rediscovering the lost essence of religion.

Yet the attempts to infuse church buildings with devotion were not particularly successful. The best-informed architects of the period, such as England's Pugin and France's Viollet le Duc studied ancient building in detail. The majority, unfortunately, simply copied things from books or from other architects. Their productions are uniformly boring. Why? For one thing, there was little sensitivity to the past periods of architecture. Components were selected from each, almost at random. The beginnings of the communication era meant that most architects could be aware of the work of others. Shared information brought with it uniformity. Nineteenth-century churches throughout Europe are quite similar. The prime model for most nineteenth-century architects was the French Gothic cathedral. Countless style-books circulated and similar forms were pasted onto buildings almost at random.

The latest technical advances also brought problems. Constructional short cuts eliminated the need for that logic of design which had determined the form of the great medieval cathedrals. It was possible to make steel pillars to hold the church up and then to box them in with machine-cut stone. The effect somehow is not 'right'.

The biggest problem with the revival of old styles is really a philosophical one. Why do we try to express ourselves with someone else's words, or make suitable places for worship with the style of another age? The uncomfortable answer, of course, is that we do not know what style is appropriate for our own age. The nineteenth century's frenetic pace of life sent traditional values tumbling in a

What are the nineteenth-century church builders trying to achieve? St Patrick's cathedral in the heart of New York (RIGHT) harks back to the fourteenth-century rather than relating to the tower blocks which now surround it.

As well as building new churches, architects carefully renovated old buildings. The Dutchman P. J. H. Cuijpers rebuilt this Romanesque church.

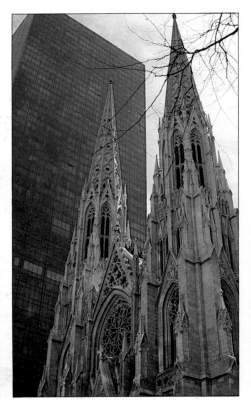

maelstrom of change. There was nothing to fill the void except imports from the past. But the imported style was stranded without its most essential support – the social and religious base on which cathedrals were built. It is for this reason that many nineteenth-century Neo-gothic, Neo-classical, or Neo-romanesque churches were never a happy experiment.

Revivalism continues in the twentieth century. There are still 'Gothic' cathedrals under construction (though very few recent commissions). The cost of completing them is now astronomical. If nothing else, they are a testament to the enduring success of their ancestors: when we think of a glorious church, the Gothic cathedral naturally comes to mind.

Despite its attempt to turn back the clock, the nineteenth century did make its own contributions to the development of church architecture. The restoration of old buildings, though over-zealous, saved many structures from dilapidation and collapse.

As the secular philosophies of the Enlightenment threatened the church, some groups responded by trying to define their doctrine more specifically. Some believed that the church should be organized differently – for example, with a group of 'non-professional' leaders rather than one full-time paid clergyman. Here the Enlightenment's emphasis on freedom had another effect; many Christians felt that if they were unhappy with existing church structures and organizations there was no reason why they should not start another church more to their liking. But these 'non-conformist' churches were not just a reaction against the established state churches. They were also a response to the renewed spiritual life that the new emphasis on evangelism was bringing to the churches.

New religious groupings produced many variations on the galleried hall-church, using iron pillars in place of stone. Some of the churches have great charm as well as a practical layout designed for the needs of the congregation. Invariably these buildings are of greater interest than the many revivalist attempts. The proliferation of small churches and chapels provided for the needs of a growing population. The multiplication of church buildings in the nineteenth century rivalled the building surge of the twelfth century. But the church itself was under attack, and putting up buildings could not shore up a crumbling institution.

Cuijpers' church of St Agatha and St Barbara at Oudenbosch (LEFT) *is a direct copy of St Peter's in Rome.*

In England and France, the nineteenth century was a time of revived interest in medieval life. Architects such as Pugin used modern techniques to recreate the atmosphere of medieval churches. This rich, dark chapel at Cheadle in England (BELOW) *gives a real sense of mystical religion.*

ODDITIES OF CHURCH DESIGN

Escaping from persecution, Christians in Göreme, Turkey, hollowed out volcanic rocks to make tiny churches and monasteries.

Every age has its dissidents, visionaries and nuts. Some start political parties or art movements; some perform feats of endurance or set out to walk around the world backwards; some build churches. They can become cult heroes or outcasts – sometimes both. History periodically reviews their achievements and decides whether they are due for revival or ridicule. The church builders either believe that they are providing for an as yet unrealized need – for example a floating church – or simply do what seems appropriate to them.

Only occasionally are their extreme forms backed by groups of Christians who actually mean to use the building. Most often these maverick buildings are the pet projects of an architect or a determined and wealthy individual. The bizarre schemes often call for unusual materials or techniques.

The Floating Church of the Redeemer for Seamen at Philadelphia was built in New York in 1851. It floated on the twin hulls of two clipper ships; its exterior was painted to resemble brown stone and inside it was complete with groined vault and bishop's throne.

At Lalibela in Ethiopia are some extraordinary seven-hundred-year-old churches built vertically downwards. They are carved out of the solid rock.

Temples or Meeting Places? Church Building Today

A group of Christians meeting today to discuss plans for a new church building has a difficult task. It is awkward enough to agree on delicate matters of budget, but it is virtually impossible to be in accord about 'style'. In a sense, there are too many options.

Regrettably, many contemporary churches seem to have been constructed primarily to look impressive – and indeed they do – rather than to meet the actual requirements of an actual worshipping congregation. Churches have been built in the shape of a fish or a crown of thorns, but these symbolic forms in no way relate to the actual practical use of the space.

Part of the problem stems from a conception of worship which makes going to church like going to the theatre or lecture hall. The word 'auditorium' is often used in reference to churches, and the personality of a preacher is too often the prime element in the service. Passive worship becomes the norm, though in fact passive worship is a contradiction in terms. The most extreme example of this is the American 'television church'. Broadcast services in America are followed by millions of viewers, many of whom would otherwise be unlikely to make the effort physically to attend church. The movements of the television camera and the studio-mixed sound of the organ can undoubtedly communicate, but these services lack the active personal contact which is so crucial to the church as a 'body of believers'.

Yet building practical and attractive churches in the modern style is possible – and preferable to attempts to cling to Gothic imitations. Invariably the modern church building which 'works' is the result of a careful review by the congregation of what the 'church' means and what elements of their life together are important. By consultation with an architect, various methods of achieving those ends can be compared. The technical possibilities of building in our century are greater than ever before. Reinforced concrete components can be made at a factory and bolted together on site. The strength of modern components means that walls no longer have to be massive. Modern building techniques are now similar to furniture making: the strength of the joints is the most critical calculation. With an internal frame of steel or pre-stressed concrete the outside of the building need not be load-bearing. It is possible to make a roof which holds up curtain-like walls of shimmering glass.

But the technical ability and the personal enthusiasm of architects has not guaranteed success. Looked at from the point of view of architecture, one reason why there is no distinctive twentieth-century 'church style' is simply that there is no distinctive twentieth-century architectural style. After the immense shock of the First World War, architects were among the most prominent voices clamouring for change. Many honestly believed that only a renewed and reconstituted environment could establish values and bring about peace. The choice, said the famous French architect Le Corbusier, is 'architecture or revolution'. It has taken us a long time to realize that their visionary utopias of architecture are only possible in a totalitarian state, and that

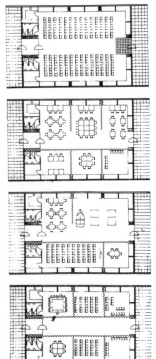

Today church buildings are designed to be used not just for use one day a week. This simple hall in the new city of Milton Keynes in England can be used for worship for 224 people, for children's activities, for film shows, a boat-building club and senior citizen's meetings.

In Asia and South America church-building has a special problem – the phenomenal rate of church growth. This church in Seoul, South Korea (LEFT) is doubling its membership every eighteen months. The main auditorium holds 11,000: six Sunday services are telecast to dozens of other buildings.

Le Corbusier's chapel of Notre Dame du Haut, one of the most famous buildings in this century, was not built for a congregation of Christians at all. It is a pilgrimage church. Inside, it seats only fifty people. The occasional vast group of pilgrims stay outside – a pulpit and altar are built on the outside wall specially for them.

The cathedral in Coventry, England, was destroyed in the Second World War. The new cathedral contains works of art by leading British artists, such as this huge crown of thorns.

A small, simple Baptist church in Stockholm, Sweden.

living in orderly ranks of tower blocks can be numbing and degrading.

After the Second World War there was a building spree of unprecedented proportions. About three-quarters of the buildings were utilitarian blocks with no pretensions to being 'architecture'. This energetic sprawl relied on the new techniques of construction, but made it painfully obvious that technical advances alone do not make for better buildings. In this period many churches were built as a kind of 'religious art' by architects who did not understand the beliefs of the congregation or the uses of the building.

The architecture of the twentieth century has no unifying style, but rather a plurality of styles. The modern freedom of choice allows a wide range of possible forms for

churches and many congregations are quite baffled when faced with the prospect of building a new church. Yet it would seem better to brave the tangles of congregational dispute than to settle for a compromise which causes no one offense but pleases no one either. Modern architecture provides scope for reinterpreting the church building as a tool for the congregation and as an emblem for the community.

The role of the church in the community is changing, too. Whilst the church is exploding in South America, Africa and South-East Asia, in the West no one is likely to call the twentieth century a particularly Christian era. But there is remarkable renewal taking place – often in unexpected ways. This renewal is bringing two things to the fore in many churches – informality

OPPOSITE, ABOVE *Christmas is celebrated at the Roman Catholic cathedral in Bristol, England. The large, low area for the congregation can be used in a variety of ways.*

No less than in other periods, today churches are built for many reasons. The Taivallahti church in Helsinki, Finland (BELOW) was designed for a competition in 1960. But as well as being an exciting construction, sunk in a rock crater, it is also an imaginatively designed meeting-place.

in worship, and a sense of community.
(Interestingly these seem to have been the
hallmark of the earliest Christian churches.)

Both these factors have had a direct effect
on church building. The boundary between
nave and chancel is now generally more
symbolic than physical. Open spaces are
often used for informal worship – even
including dance. Many congregations also
use their buildings for more than just
housing the weekly worship service. Some
function as community centres and schools
during the week, others provide libraries,
study rooms, lounges and space for regular
communal meals. The policy of some
congregations is that if the church grows
larger than two hundred people, another
church is begun so that close personal
contact can be maintained. Such a young

congregation might meet in a home, a school hall or a converted shop until it outgrows them.

Church building today is characterized by its great variety. Basilica types, ovals, cross plans, free form – there are few 'rules'. This willingness to experiment with form has been particularly significant for church building in the Third World. Here the traditional 'Western' forms have no roots, but local building methods and styles offer many new possibilities.

A church building is not 'the church'. But an imaginative and considered architecture can be a useful and attractive tool for the work of the church. The history of church building demonstrates that the urge to express faith through architecture is basic. The quality of church architecture depends on many factors, not least the sensitivity and dedication of the congregation concerned in assessing its role in the community. As society changes the church needs to apply the gifts and skills of its members to finding new means of expressing its life. It needs to listen, look and learn. The exploration of churches past and present can not only give pleasure but also help cultivate an alertness of what the church is called to be.

The spectacular Crystal Cathedral in California is a product of the US 'electronic church', built from $20 million donations received from vast TV audiences. It is designed in the shape of a four-cornered star to make an impressive backdrop for the TV messages delivered each Sunday from the marble pulpit.

Christians meet together to worship God in a variety of ways (CENTRE). *Purpose-designed buildings help, but they are not indispensible, as the persecuted church in the Soviet Union* (BELOW) *has shown.*

GLOSSARY

Ambulatory aisle around the chancel used for processions.
Ashlar blocks of masonry with smoothed, squared surfaces. Also called 'dressed stone'.
Ambo raised lectern, often used in medieval Italian churches, from which the Bible was read.
Apse vaulted semi-circular east end of a chancel or chapel.
Aisle side areas running parallel to the nave.
Altar table or stone slab on supports used for celebration of the Eucharist.
Arch structural support between two columns or piers made in an inverted curve.
Arcade range of arches carried on columns or piers.
Aumbry cupboard or recess used for storing cups and plates used in the Eucharist.

Bay section of wall between pillars. Generally a nave consists of a succession of bays, each with the same combination of windows and columns.
Bema raised platform in early churches, on which preacher stood to speak.
Blind (as in 'blind tracery', 'blind arcade', etc.) decorative feature applied to the surface of a wall rather than standing free.
Boss ornamental knob covering the intersection of ribs in a vault or ceiling.

Baptistry building or section of the church used for baptisms; or a baptism pool.
Basilica early style of church, consisting of a nave and two or more lower, narrower aisles.
Buttress brick or stonework built against a wall to give it support.

Capital top crowning feature of a column or pier.
Carrel (or carol) niche in a cloister, designed for a monk to sit in and work.
Chancel eastern end of a church, sometimes reserved for the clergy and choir.
Chevron Romanesque decoration in form of a zig-zag.
Chapter house assembly room in a monastery or cathedral used for discussion of business.
Choir area of the church where the services are sung.
Churrigueresque florid, highly-decorated late Baroque style, found particularly in Spain and Mexico.
Clerestory upper level of the nave wall, pierced by windows.
Cloisters external quadrangle surrounded by a covered walkway.
Column vertical load-bearing shaft with circular cross-section, usually slightly tapered.
Compound pier upright support comprised of a cluster of shafts, not necessarily attached to each other.
Corbel projecting stone block which supports a beam.
Cornice topmost decorative moulded section surmounting a

column. Also any projecting moulding at the roof level of a building.
Corinthian order: see ORDER.
Crypt space beneath the main floor of a church.

Diaperwork ornamental pattern of repeated lozenges or squares.
Dogtooth early English and Norman ornamental pattern consisting of series of three-dimensional star-like shapes.
Dome vault built on a circular base.
Dressed stone see ASHLAR.
Drum round vertical wall supporting a dome.

Elevation square-on 'flat' view of the back, front or side of a building.
Entablature uppermost part of the 'order' surmounting a column. Consists of cornice, frieze and architrave.
Engaged shaft see HALF SHAFT.

Facing finish material applied to the outside of a building.
Fan vault see VAULT.
Finial ornament at the tip of a spire, pinnacle or canopy.

Flamboyant late Gothic style in France, characterized by wavy lines of tracery.
Flying buttress buttress in form of arch, supporting upper portion of wall.

Gallery (or tribune) upper storey inside a church, above the aisle, open to the nave.
Gargoyle water spout projecting from a roof, often carved as a head or figure.
Groin vault see VAULT.
Grisaille stained glass with mostly white glass in small lozenge-shaped panes painted in decorative patterns.

Half shaft shaft or column partially attached to or let into a wall. Also called 'engaged shaft'.
Hall church church in which nave and aisles are about the same height.

Iconostasis screen in a Byzantine church which separates the nave from the sanctuary, usually with three doors and covered with images (icons).
Icon image of a saint, apostle or martyr used as an aid for worship of God especially in Eastern churches.

Iconoclasm opposition to the veneration of religious images.
Ionic order see ORDER.

Keystone central stone in an arch or rib.

Lancet window narrow window with a pointed arch.
Lady chapel chapel dedicated to the Virgin Mary, often at the east end of the church.
Lantern circular or polygonal tower topping a dome or roof.
Lights openings between the mullions of a window.
Lintel horizontal timber or stone beam.

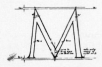

Martyrion memorial or church building constructed over the grave of a martyr.
Misericord bracket on the underside of the hinged seat of the choir stall, provided for monks to lean against while standing through long services.
Mouldings contoured shaping given to projecting elements such as arches, lintels, string courses, etc.
Mullion wooden or stone framework within a window.

Narthex vestibule across the west end of a church.
Nave main middle section of the inside of a church running from the west end to the crossing.

Ogee arch see ARCH.
Order combination of columns, base, capitals, and entablature developed in ancient Rome and Greece and extensively copied in periods of classical revival. The most usual orders are Doric, Ionic and Corinthian.

Pediment gently pitched gable above a portico.
Pier solid vertical masonry support with non-circular cross-section.
Pilaster shallow pier or squared column attached to a wall.
Pinnacle small tower-like top to a spire, buttress, etc.
Piscina basin in a niche, used for washing the vessels used in the Eucharist.
Plinth projecting base of a wall.
Portico entrance in the form of a open or partially-enclosed roofed space.

Pyx container in which the bread consecrated for the Eucharist is kept. It is often elaborately carved or decorated.

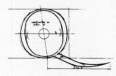

Quoins dressed stones at the corner of a building, often protruding slightly from the face of the wall.

Reredos raised decorated screen behind the communion table.
Retro-choir area behind the communion table in a cathedral.
Rib projecting stone or brickwork on a ceiling or vault, usually load-bearing.
Rood the old Saxon word for cross. Crucifix attached to a 'rood beam' and usually flanked by images of saints.
Rood screen screen below the rood separating the chancel from the nave, sometimes substantial enough to carry a 'rood loft', or gallery.

Sanctuary area around the communion table at the east end of a church.

Sedilia seats for the clergy built into the south wall of the chancel.
Spire tall conical or polygonal structure built on top of a tower.
Squinch arches placed diagonally across the corner of an intersection of walls to carry a tower, drum, or dome.
Stalls row of carved wooden or stone seats in the choir.
Steeple combination of tower and spire.
Strainer arch see ARCH.
String course projecting moulded horizontal band of stonework.

Tabernacle ornamental receptacle or recess to contain relics or the sacraments used in the Eucharist.
Transept transverse arms of a cross-shaped church.
Tribune gallery above the aisle in some cathedrals.
Triforium middle level of nave between the arcade and clerestory.
Tracery ornamental shaped stone or woodword in windows or screens.
Tympanum area between the lintel of a doorway and the arch above it, usually decorated.

Vault arched ceiling. There are several types of vault – the barrel (or tunnel) vault, the groin vault, the lierne vault and the quadrapartite vault.